learning in later life

learning in laterlife

an introduction for educators & carers

PETER JARVIS

**KOGAN
PAGE**

To my wife, Maureen, who spends a great deal of her life working with those in the fourth age, and in memory of my parents-in-law Edris and Arthur Hubbard (lessons from whose lives also appear in this book).

First published in 2001

Kogan Page Limited
120 Pentonville Road
London N1 9JN

© Peter Jarvis, 2001

British Library Cataloguing in Publication Data

A CIP record for this book is available from the British Library.

ISBN 0 7494 3398 1

Typeset by Jean Cussons Typesetting, Diss, Norfolk
Printed and bound in Great Britain by Clays Ltd, St Ives plc

Contents

The author

Peter Jarvis is Professor of Continuing Education in the School of Educational Studies at the University of Surrey, where he is also convenor of the Centre for Research in Lifelong Learning. He is also adjunct professor of adult education at the University of Georgia, in the United States. In addition, he teaches sociology, part-time, for the Open University. He holds degrees from the Universities of London, Sheffield, Birmingham, Aston and Surrey and was awarded an honorary doctorate from the University of Helsinki. He is also a Fellow of the Royal Society of Arts. In 1990, he was awarded a scholarship by the Japan Society for the Promotion of Science at the University of Tokyo.

His work, having sociological and philosophical foundations, has focused mainly on aspects of the education of adults and lifelong learning. He has taught teacher, vocational, and continuing education and has undertaken research in adult learning and a number of other projects. He has also been involved in distance education for many years.

In 1988, he was awarded the Cyril O. Houle World Award for Literature in Adult Education by the American Association of Adult and Continuing Education. He was also awarded the Comenius Award of the European Society for Voluntary Associations in 1997 and, in the same year, was conducted into the International Hall of Fame in America.

He is the author of many books. Amongst his latest are *Adult and Continuing Education: Theory and Practice* (second edition, Routledge 1995), *Ethics and the Education of Adults in Late Modern Society* (NIACE, 1997), *International Dictionary of Adult and Continuing Education* (second edition, Kogan Page, 1998) and *The Practitioner Researcher: Developing Theory from Practice* (Jossey Bass, 1999). He has also recently written *The Human Resources Handbook* (with Pat Hargreaves, Kogan Page, 1998) and *Theory and Practice of Learning* (with John Holford and Colin Griffin, Kogan Page, 1998). He has also written many papers and chapters in books and his work has been widely translated.

He is the founding editor of *The International Journal of Lifelong Education* and serves on the editorial boards of a number of journals. He is a frequent speaker and lecturer on adult, continuing and higher education, and lifelong learning, in many parts of the world.

Foreword

Occasionally a book comes into being that crystallizes a discipline that has been developing in slow motion. *Learning in Later Life* by Peter Jarvis is such a text: it ties together major strands of theory and research that have emerged in the past 20 years and presents old age as a time of opportunity and development. This is in direct contrast to the perspective that old age is a period of obsolescence and decline. Ours is a new age for growing old, a time of potential and a time to explore what Jarvis says is the 'relationship between learning, living and ageing'. This book contains several exciting new ideas in both academic and practical spheres. Its initial thesis is that in later life, rather than in adult education aimed at employability and vocation, one needs a 'learning therapist'. The vocation, so to speak, is the person in a state of self-identity and a search for meaning. In the third age (defined as 50 to 74 years old), one explores rituals of separation and new post-retirement opportunities. Jarvis states that freedom, autonomy and authenticity are the centrepieces of discovery. Furthermore, in the fourth age (after 75), there is much personal significance and creativity available.

The book is shaped holistically, presented in a lifecycle perspective. It sets out to explore how learning occurs, and connects original research by the author to growth and development in the last part of the lifespan. Chapter 1 discusses the emergence of education for adults from its roots as a religious occupation, a primarily middle-class female pursuit. Jarvis traces the history of adult education in the United States and the United Kingdom, and the development of third age education during the past 30 years. He highlights the potential for cognitive development that exists when older adults are challenged. As changes in vocational education occur throughout the lifespan, globalization and the need for retirement education opportunities for lifelong learning emerge. The book takes the argument that now, in the new millennium, the time has come to explore the way that human growth and lifelong learning intersect.

In Chapter 2, 'Learning and the learning society', Professor Jarvis delves further into the process of learning. Implications for building reflective and conscious interactions in formal and self-directed circumstances are explored. Thoughtful educators will see the 'learning society' as a model for all ages. As Jarvis points out, learning is essential to all of us who must adapt and transform to the new challenges of life. So it follows that Chapter 3 is called 'Learning, being and ageing'. It is an overview of the optimization theory of cognitive development: learning is viewed as an ontological process with spiritual implications. Through learning, humans can transcend and transform their environment. One thinks of the following quote from Henri Bergson:

> To exist is to change;
> To change is to mature;
> To mature is to
> Create oneself endlessly.

Chapter 3 includes a basic map of developmentalism that frames the literature of gerontological education. It reflects the author's thesis that learning is an opportunity to become more integrated. This is perhaps the richest chapter for the practitioner who trusts in the maturing process as a way of finding meaning in the culture; it explores the deepening potential for cognitive and effective growth in which ego developmentalists have invested in the past quarter of a century. It is fitting that Jarvis refers to the work of Jane Loevinger who observed, 'The striving to master, to integrate, to make sense of experience is not one ego function among many, but the essence of the ego.' Indeed, the role of biography – and autobiography – that has become central to the literature of life review and reminiscence continues to grow as more and more elders seek to make sense of 'who we are'.

Chapter 4, 'Learning from experience and experienced learners', is a postmodern analysis of the nature of sense-making within our time. Jarvis's discussion of multiple intelligences, of the research on fluid and crystallized intelligence, and of the nature of experienced learners within the educational experience, is concise and direct. It reviews what classroom strategies work in learning situations with older people. Therefore, Chapter 5, 'Learning to retire', presents the symbolic and ritualistic passage that many older adults experience. Surely this transition cries out for continuing education. As practitioners and counsellors, clergy and older adults, we need to explore this rich landscape of a growing terrain in the culture. As greater numbers of citizens arrive at 'seniorhood', we are fortunate to have a text to support their intellectual and emotional maturity.

Chapters 6 to 10 focus on the specific curricula and nature of learning as one grows into maturity. They are: 'Learning after retirement'; 'Learning new work roles'; 'Learning meaning and wisdom'; 'Learning spirituality'; and 'Learning mental fitness'. These chapters, rich in theory and detail, point to the possibilities that education holds for all people, despite age and background. The concept of 'learning therapist' resonates with meaning here as we contemplate participating in the continued renewal and integration of mature minds. There are no limits and no rules: there is only the positive message that self-initiated discovery and freely-chosen post-retirement education have unlimited potential to provide authenticity, autonomy and freedom.

Chapter 11, 'Learning in the fourth age', provides guidance for those working with elders over the age of 75. Again, Jarvis provides models for continued learning and the empowerment of elders. Specific techniques such as programmatic direction, reminiscence and life history work, and sensitive communication with confused individuals, are given. Jarvis underlines the nature of individualized approaches, the need for interpersonal relationships, and finally, the nature of personal identity for the dying. This section encourages practitioners to trust their own sense of caring as they develop learning experiences for elders. Chapter 12 builds on this construct, leaving the reader with a rich moral imperative to create so that others can experience their fullest selves. Jarvis's notion that a construction of a learning society is essential to our new lifespan imperative is a sound and thoughtful one, backed with theoretical and research underpinnings.

This is a wonderfully human book. Anyone who works with older adults will be fascinated by *Learning in Later Life*. In a funny way, older adults – because they are becoming closer to death – are actually closer to life. For many, the means to life is what we commonly call 'education'. As they come to terms with meaning, older adults sort through their experiences, they integrate, they focus. How lucky the practitioner who encounters these older learners! We are fortunate to have a book that takes a fresh look at this phenomenon. Rather than seeing old age as a period of obsolescence and decline, we have ample scholarly support for the prescription for intellectual growth and emotional maturity. It is a brave new world, indeed.

Mary Alice Wolf,
Professor of Gerontology and
Director, Institute in Gerontology
Saint Joseph College, West Hartford,
Connecticut 06117, USA

Preface

Learning in later life has become a commonplace phrase in recent years; government ministers use the term and there are learning in later life networks. The fact that it has become such an accepted term does demonstrate that the fact that older people can continue their learning is no longer a novel idea. Yet the implications of it are not really very apparent. When government ministers use the term, they seem to imply that learning has to do with employability. That is how they also use the term 'learning' – although, to be fair, in all the government reports on learning there has been reference to non-work learning and even once to the idea of learning about the spiritual dimension. However, the implications of human learning have not been thoroughly worked out in government policy, but neither have they been systematically worked out in the literature of lifelong education.

Once the educational and policy emphases are put on human learning and the learner, rather than on education, there is a different set of implications. These relate to the fact that learning is not only for life, but it is about the very processes of living. But learning and living in later life, especially in the third and fourth ages, may be very different from learning and living for younger people. However, it is the latter group who define agendas and policies, and they often do so from a very limited understanding of human learning – an understanding still restricted by the imperfect behaviourist and cognitivist definitions that have pervaded education for the past few decades.

This is a book about learning throughout the whole of the human life. It demonstrates clearly that helping others learn is not only the job of the educator, but of all who care. Consequently, a new role of learning therapist is advocated in the book where the role of facilitating learning in all situations in which the elderly find themselves is explored. All educators should be carers and carers should be learning therapists, but there should be some for whom this is a specialist role and so the book closes with a brief chapter examining some of the things that might be included in professional continuing education courses for all the caring professions.

This book starts from an experiential understanding of learning, based on a

research project that I undertook into adult learning, and its implications are gradually worked out through to the last stages of life. The first chapters contain a
report of the research project and a full theoretical understanding of the relationship between learning, living and ageing. In the fifth chapter, retirement is
discussed and then issues relating to learning after work are examined, including
attending education classes, such as adult education classes and the Universities of
the Third Age, and volunteering and mentoring. However, learning about
meaning, wisdom and spirituality are also examined. In Chapters 10 and 11,
learning is discussed in relation to physical and mental well-being and, finally, its
place in relation to dementia, Alzheimer's disease, and the last stages of life is
analysed. This book, then, is written for:

● educators of adults, especially those who work with older learners;
● carers, doctors and nurses who work with the elderly;
● therapists, both occupational therapists and physiotherapists;
● those who own or work in residential homes;
● clergy and volunteers;
● students preparing to enter these professions and for post-graduates special-
  izing in studies in later life;
● those who are in later life.

I first became involved with working with the elderly when I attended a
residential college for a year. The college was situated in a small village in
Derbyshire. It was rather like a folk high school, and each student was allocated
a work task for each day. Mine was to visit a retired tutor from the college and
his wife each weekday afternoon in order to help them around the home. The
retired tutor had Parkinson's disease and, working with them, I learnt at first
hand about some of the problems of being old and infirm and living in rural
England. When I was an undergraduate I visited a residential home for the elderly
every week and became responsible for organizing the work of the university
college in that home. Thereafter, I worked as a Methodist minister for six years
and a great deal of the emphasis of my work was with the elderly in the
community.
    When I left the circuit ministry for higher education, I did not lose my
concerns for the elderly and, as an educator of adults, over the years I have written
a number of papers on third age education. Indeed, I have extracted occasional
points from some of these in this book. However, I have deliberately not referenced any of them here as I have developed ideas from them in this book,
although I have referenced other books that I have written. I have also organized
international third age conferences at the University of Surrey, where I have also
taught an Educational Gerontology module on a Masters degree. I have also been
privileged to speak at other third age conferences, including the International
Association of Third Age Universities bi-annual conference in Germany in 1998.

I have been the learner in my interactions with third agers and I hope that some of what I have learnt is reflected in this current study.

While this is an academic book, it also examines many practical issues since I do not believe that there should be a divide between theory and practice. Indeed, practice should – and does – precede theory in many instances. Consequently, I hope that this book proves to be useful to those who read it, and that it will contribute to widening the debate about learning, especially learning in later life.

1

Learning and third age education

This is an ageing society – it is widely accepted now that in Western Europe and the United States, amongst other places, the older population comprises an ever increasing proportion of the whole. Demographics indicate that the population in the United Kingdom is ageing and that by the year 2001, 15 million people will fall within the age group 50–74 years and a further 4.4 million will be 75 years plus. Significantly, only 12.6 million will be under 16 years old and 27.1 million will be between 16 and 49 years old (Annual Abstract of Statistics, cited from Carnegie Inquiry, 1993, p 115). Consequently, it may be seen that third agers (those between 50 and 74 years) constitute a significant proportion of the population. A similar phenomenon may be detected throughout Europe and the United States. Sheehy (1995) actually regards 50 years old as the beginning of second adulthood! It is upon this age group that this study concentrates, with 'elder' being defined as being 50 years of age and older. It is also the age at which many companies begin to invite employees to consider early retirement – and enter the third age.

It is not to be denied that for many elders, the third age has become a time of leisure – even if it has sometimes been enforced! Significantly, employment and economic activity rates for older workers (those aged 55 to 64) have fallen over the past 20 years. Indeed, in the United Kingdom approximately 91.3 per cent of all men were economically active in 1971, but by the year 1988 it was only 68.4 per cent (OECD [Organisation for Economic Cooperation and Development] cited from Carnegie Inquiry, 1993, p 19), and it was still decreasing. By contrast, economic activity among older women has increased, but only in part-time work.

In the United States there are now more people over 65 years of age than there are teenagers. Even an ex-President of the United States can write a book on *The Virtues of Aging* (Carter, 1998). But this is also a learning society, and the number of educational institutions for older adults is increasing much more rapidly than is the number of schools! Indeed, in the Finnish European Union Presidency

Seminar in 1999, third age learning was regarded as one of the eight major educational issues to be discussed.

Learning in later life has become something of a catchphrase in recent years and there is an assumption that it relates in some way to third age education. Government documents certainly seem to include third age education within its strategy for making the United Kingdom a learning society. The way in which this assumption is made is challenged in this book, although I certainly do not want to deny that third age education is a part of learning in later life. Learning occurs in formal, non-formal and informal situations – something we shall discuss more thoroughly in the second chapter. Education, however, is learning in a formal situation but does not include learning in other life situations. In this sense, the study of third age education is both a sub-discipline of education for adults and also of gerontology, and in this chapter the focus is on the manner in which educational gerontology has emerged and how it relates to the education of adults. Thereafter, we shall examine the learning processes and how they relate to later life in general. Naturally, this will include considerable reference to adult education both in the UK and in the United States, where there have been many innovations in later life learning.

As early as 1962, the Institute for Retired Professionals was founded in New York under the sponsorship of the New School for Social Research and this became the first Institute for Learning in Retirement, which has subsequently become the Elderhostel Institute Network. Ten years later, the University of the Third Age was founded in Toulouse, in France, and these universities have spread very rapidly throughout Europe and around the rest of the world. At the International Association of Third Age Universities (AIUTA), meeting in Germany in 1998, there were representatives from 18 different countries. Other networks and groups have also appeared more recently, including TALIS (Third Age Learning International Studies) and two journals exist devoted to the study of third age education.

Older people are undertaking learning opportunities in considerable numbers and the study of their education, educational gerontology, is also beginning to emerge. It might be viewed as part of the wider study of lifelong learning, or even more specifically as a sub-section of the study of the education of adults. Indeed, it is suggested here that third age education is a mirror of non-vocational adult education a generation ago and we shall trace this through this chapter, which is divided into three sections: the emergence of education for adults; changing fields of study; third age education. The chapter then concludes by focusing upon learning rather than on education.

The emergence of education for adults

There are many comprehensive histories of adult education (Harrison, 1961,

Kelly, 1970, Fieldhouse, 1996 for the UK, Knowles, 1977 and Kett, 1994 for the United States, *inter alia*) and so it is not my intention to provide a full overview of the way that adult education emerged in the UK, the United States or anywhere else. Nevertheless, it is necessary to focus upon some aspects of this development in order to illustrate the thesis of this chapter.

As general education developed after the Enlightenment, children were schooled to receive that knowledge which the older generation considered sufficiently valuable to be passed on to the succeeding generation. Education was, in fact, defined by Emile Durkheim (1956, p 71) as 'the influence exercised by adult generations on those who are not yet ready for social life'. For most children, their education was completed in their teenage years, although a minority continued their initial education to the end of their university career. Vocational training, or education, followed immediately after initial education and young people entered employment. At this point, all education terminated. There was little vocational training after the initial preparation. Indeed, at this time there was a general belief that adults could not learn a great deal more, since it was widely believed that mental decline set in by the time individuals had reached their middle twenties.

However, people gradually began to realize that adults could actually continue to learn (see Knox, 1977 for a summary of this research). The emergence of adult education was, therefore, a totally new phenomenon in as much as it was not connected in any way with initial education or vocational training. There was a clearly demarcated boundary between them. Adult education was distinct and assumed a non-vocational perspective. Much of the early adult education was religious in nature (Kelly, 1970). It was also optional and voluntary, non-accredited and, by and large, a middle-class leisure time pursuit. The middle classes had the necessary educational background and cultural capital to continue their education. In addition, since it was non-vocational it appeared to be a pursuit that was undertaken by those who were not in employment, so that women predominated in adult education classes. There was also a genuine concern about seeking to reach out to those who did not come to adult education classes and attract them to classes. It had many of the characteristics of a social movement with a strong mission to offer knowledge to those who were not so well educated. It assumed many of the characteristics of an idealistic enterprise 'learning for learning's sake'. However, like initial education and vocational training, it merely reproduced the social and cultural conditions of the day. Additionally, like initial education (eg Bowles and Gintis, 1976), it was criticized for its inherently conservative nature, and later more radical adult educators emerged, pointing out that education is never neutral and always manifests itself as a political phenomenon (eg Freire, 1972). Other radical and feminist forms of adult education were also espoused – see Keddie (1980) and Thompson (1983).

The academic study of the education of adults also emerged during this period, with the first professor of adult education being appointed at Nottingham University in 1920 and the first PhD in adult education being awarded to Basil

Yeaxlee by the University of London in 1925. Eleven years later, Teachers College, Columbia University, was to award the first PhD in adult education in the United States. By the 1960s and 1970s, the study of adult education was becoming established in both countries and once this had occurred, the training of adult educators as distinct from the preparation of school teachers began to appear. But just as this was happening other changes were to occur that were to have profound changes on adult education.

It was in the 1960s and 1970s that changes in the nature of society were emerging. Stehr (1994, pp 5–17) provides an overview of some of the theories of the development of the knowledge society. The significance of this is quite profound for the structure of work, since Reich (1991) suggests that in the 1950s there were probably no more than 8 per cent of the US workforce that might be classified as knowledge workers but, by the time he wrote his book, this proportion had increased to 20 per cent. And it would continue to increase. But as this process has continued, so there has been a great demand for knowledge workers to gain *more* knowledge, often through in-service courses initially, but also by returning to education in order to gain further qualifications. Other occupations have also changed and new ones have emerged, and these changes have completely transformed the socio-economic class structure of contemporary society. With all these developments, further education and training has also become more necessary, and human resource development has become a fashionable term. Consequently, there has been a tremendous expansion of higher education and higher education for further qualifications. Indeed, Campbell (1984, p 14) notes that 'in 1974–75, adult learners in credit and formal non-credit courses in Canada became the new majority within the universities' clientele'.

However, this process has been exacerbated by globalization, since countries now have to compete in a world market to produce an increasing number of products to sell competitively on the world stage. This competitive climate has resulted in a continued increase in knowledge workers and also other structural changes in employment – a career, for many people, is no longer progression in the same occupation until retirement. Jobs are changing – new jobs are appearing and increasingly new forms of training are being introduced and, significantly, these have occurred throughout the whole of the work life. In addition, individuals without employment need the opportunity to be trained in order to be able to return to work – and unemployment education has become a major welfare provision in many Western societies.

Vocational education was now no longer something that occurred at the start of a career, but something that continued throughout the whole of the working life. Government reports now emphasize the significance of knowledge for work. For instance, the European Union's report on the learning society (1995, p 3) specified the 'need for a broad knowledge base... designed to build up abilities for employment'. While the report also recognized the significance of general education, its emphasis was primarily on knowledge for employment.

In the United Kingdom, as expenditure on the welfare state has been curtailed, so the quite generously funded adult education of the 1970s has been restricted. Now non-vocational adult education courses are funded differently, if at all, from vocational education. The Kennedy Report (1997, pp 33–34) recognized this difference, although it pleaded for more equal recognition, and in the more recent White Paper (1999), *Learning to Succeed*, this was recognized. However, many subjects that were once classified as non-vocational and were non-accredited have now been reclassified as vocational and accredited, so that funding can be sought and enrolment fees kept lower.

Thus we can see that, with the emergence of the knowledge society and the process of globalization, the nature of vocational education has changed. What was previously education and training of young people before they entered the workforce has become education for the whole of the work life. While the more traditional forms of non-vocational adult education remain, they have become marginalized in adulthood. At the centre of education of adults at the end of the twentieth century is vocational adult education. General adult education is being marginalized, and those more radical formulations of adult education even more marginalized (where they have not disappeared altogether) even though there may be an even greater need for them now than ever before.

Significantly, and almost ironically, as work has become the centre of many people's lives, to such an extent that some individuals appear to have allowed it to pervade the whole of their lives, people are living a lot longer. There is now a need for preparation for the long leisure years that confront retirees. Pre-retirement education courses have become increasingly popular, helping people to prepare for their leisure time and also helping them to consider the significance of life beyond work. Many of these have worked with knowledge for much of their working lives so that they are likely candidates for post-retirement education. But before we look at education for those who have retired, it is necessary to return to the study of the education for adults since it is there that we can trace these changes most clearly.

Changing fields of study

As we review these historical developments, we can see that the fields of study of the education of adults have also changed, and that academic debates have ensued. For instance, in the early days of adult education, it was something quite different from other forms of education – indeed, the prefix 'adult' was sufficient to demarcate it from education. However, as early at 1929 the term 'lifelong education' put in its first appearance (Yeaxlee, 1929) – but it did not gain popularity in the inter-war years. Even though UNESCO adopted the concept after the Second World War with far-sighted thinkers like Lengrand (1975) and members of the OECD promulgating the idea, the time was not really right for the concept to be adopted. The idea of a boundary between school education and adult education was still too strong.

However, in the 1970s, that boundary was being breached and the idea was emerging of continuing education, and by the mid-1980s in the United Kingdom the concept of adult education was subsumed within continuing education. At first there was a sub-division between continuing education and continuing professional education but, as we have seen above, non-vocational education was marginalized and continuing education became dominated by continuing vocational education. However, continuing education was not to retain its prevalence for long because by the 1990s, the idea of lifelong education was rediscovered. But the focus of this was also to change – for society had become a globalized market and education itself was being commodified. This commodification process had been speeded up by the introduction of distance education and information technology. Now the emphasis was on learning and it became possible to purchase learning materials – and so the focus became learning and the dominant concept lifelong learning, since learners no longer needed the formalized educational system in order to learn.

Naturally, learning in later life fits nicely into the idea of lifelong learning and it might appear that it has been accepted without a great deal of difficulty. But this has not been the case, as is illustrated from the terminological debate of the period.

In the 1960s, when Malcolm Knowles (1970) first popularized the idea of andragogy in the United States, he sub-titled his book 'Andragogy versus Pedagogy' reflecting the clear-cut distinction between the two forms of education. But this was immediately disputed by some scholars, so that in the revised edition the sub-title became 'From Pedagogy to Andragogy' (Knowles, 1980). However, third age education did not find its place in andragogy, and so the term gerogogy emerged (Label, 1978). Such divisions were not popular with all adult educators and by 1979 the term 'humanagogy' (Knudson, 1979) was being suggested in the United States, pointing to the idea of lifelong education. Unbeknown to the US scholars engaged in this terminological debate, similar terms actually existed in parts of Europe, some of which had a far longer history – and there is a series of books still published in Germany, edited by Franz Poggeler, entitled *Studies in Pedagogy, Andragogy and Gerontogogy*. The boundaries between adult education and third age education are, therefore, still reflected in this title, although the US debate 20 years earlier indicated the fact that, in the United States at least, boundaries between initial education, adult education and third age education were being lowered.

Now it might be argued, in most parts of the Western world, that the idea of lifelong learning, within which might be included lifelong education, has now become widely accepted. But as we have already noted, the idea of lifelong education still contains the dominant idea of vocational education so that the idea of third age education still lies at the margins, even though it is a rapidly developing field of lifelong education. And it is to this that we must now turn our attention.

Third age education

As we have noted, third age education really started between 1962 and 1972 and within the past quarter of a century it has grown and assumed a most significant place within the lives of many older adults. Third age education has assumed different structures in different parts of the world. In the United States much of it has taken one of two forms: Institutes for Learning in Retirement, which are attached to the universities but which also had their own network, and Elderhostel. However, in 1988, the Institute Network merged with Elderhostel to form the Elderhostel Institute Network, but Elderhostel itself is still regarded as separate from its institutional educational arm.

In Europe, the Universities of the Third Age (U3As) have assumed two forms: the first form (favoured by many continental European countries) attaches U3As to the local universities from which they receive support; and in the second form in the United Kingdom (and also Australia and New Zealand) the U3As are separate from the universities and are voluntary autonomous organizations in their own right.

In reality, however, this division is not quite as clear-cut geographically at it appears here and there are, for instance, third age education institutes in universities, such as at Strathclyde in Scotland. These educational organizations have become rather like social movements with a middle-class basis, campaigning for education for older persons, and reaching out to those people less fortunate than themselves and offering them an opportunity to pursue their learning, thus reflecting the way that liberal adult education has developed.

In precisely the same manner as other adults had to demonstrate, or have proven, that they could continue to learn after schooling, so third agers have had to demonstrate, or have proven, that they can continue to learn well into their very old age. This has probably been harder to do since the incidence of mental decline in third, and more significantly, fourth ages is well documented. Even so, there have been clear indications that older people's crystallized intelligence can continue to increase well into old age (see Knox, 1977) and, by 1978, Gisela Labouvie-Vief (1978, p 249) concluded about third age education that 'much of what we know about the educability of adults is in need of revision'. More recently, Cusack and Thompson (1998) have been advocating mental fitness and Paggi and Hayslip (1999) have been utilizing forms of mental aerobics in order to enhance the self-esteem of older adults through engaging together in sophisticated mental exercises in groups, and we shall return to these in the later parts of this book. Gradually, it is becoming accepted that the mind does not necessarily cease to function when individuals retire from work. People can still enjoy their leisure time learning. Indeed, there is growing evidence that education actually helps to protect the mind against decline in cognitive functioning.

Carlton and Soulsby (1999) record a number of instances about what being able to learn means to older people and these stories can be replicated by almost anybody who has been involved in teaching adults, especially older adults. Learning helps broaden the mind, retain active interests, and so forth. It is a great benefit to many – but, as we shall see later, there might come a stage in some people's lives where they no longer seek it.

Consequently, we have witnessed this tremendous growth in third age education – but most of it is for leisure time since not all older adults want to pursue education for qualifications. Indeed, there is a growing advocacy for third age education (Elmore, 1999). They are interested in those subjects that have traditionally been studied in middle-class non-vocational adult education (Carlton and Soulsby, 1999, p 26), although some still wish to pursue subjects that might be classified as vocational. What we are seeing, therefore, is that the liberal adult education curriculum of the previous generation has now become the menu for third age learning. More significantly, much of the vocabulary and many of the concerns about third age education are the concerns that were being expressed by adult educators about non-vocational adult education, eg provision, barriers to learning, motivation and attitudes, advice and guidance.

However, as third age education is reflecting non-vocational adult education of a generation ago, a number of questions need to be asked about it:

- As this older generation is the one that grew up with the increasing popularity of non-vocational adult education, is this current growth of third age education merely a reflection of the same concerns that the people had when they were younger?
- How will third age education develop when those people who have worked in the knowledge occupations all their lives retire?
- Will the notion of liberal adult education be transformed with the emergence of the same types of radical education that emerged in non-vocational education?
- Will a research agenda emerge and will third agers conduct their own research into educational and learning needs?
- What about learning in the fourth age?

As yet there are no signs that the more radical perspectives in adult education are emerging in third age education. However, if the third agers are increasingly marginalized and their living conditions compared to those in work lowered, then the small radical movement currently present among seniors might find its way into adult education and new forms of radical adult education might emerge. This might be even more significant for radical feminist adult education, since women tend to live longer than men do and also tend to be more impoverished.

Finally, the training of adult educators has developed rapidly over the past 30 years and so it might be asked whether those people who work with older adults, such as educators, therapists, clergy, and all other health care professionals, need training in adult learning. Clearly, evidence is emerging that even people suffering from certain forms of dementia can recover a great deal of their independence if they engage in learning exercises. Indeed, a new occupation of learning therapists might begin to appear and a new dimension to the caring relationship has become evident – we will discuss this in the final chapters of the book. New training courses might need to be devised that teach therapists how to organize mental aerobics and other such mental and physical exercises in order to revolutionize the type of care that older adults receive and enrich their lives.

Conclusion

As third age education is developing, we can see many parallels with non-vocational adult education. Indeed, it might be claimed that this form of adult education has been reinvented in third age education. It is, therefore, necessary that those who are currently developing third age education look back at the history of non-vocational education to ensure that they neither reinvent the wheel nor make the same mistakes the non-vocational adult educators have made in the past. Even so, history does not repeat itself completely, so that this is a new educational phenomenon and a further manifestation of lifelong learning. Indeed, it is a new form of non-vocational adult education. However, the one major conceptual shift in the past decade has been from education to learning – and so it is now necessary to analyse the concept of learning.

2
Learning and the learning society

As we saw in the previous chapter, learning has traditionally been associated with institutions of education, schools and colleges, and so on. It is only recently that education has been subsumed within learning, that it has become widely recognized that 'you can teach an old dog new tricks' and learning has become associated with something that is lifelong. Previously the study of learning was regarded as either the research preserve of educationalists or psychologists – but certainly not gerontologists. But this book has been written not only for those who study later life – but for all those who work, or intend to work, with older people – educationalists, therapists, nurses and doctors, others in health care, the clergy, and even the older volunteers who work with the elderly. Let me start by saying that learning should not be regarded as the exclusive preserve of any single discipline or practice – learning is about living – it is an existential phenomenon. Throughout this book, learning will be viewed as a necessary condition for normal human life and we will identify different forms of learning in relation to living and to the formal educational system.

The argument underlying the book is that learning is a complex set of processes which people undertake at every age throughout life. *Learning is the process whereby human beings create and transform experiences into knowledge, skills, attitudes, beliefs, values, senses and emotions.* It is at the very heart of our humanity. We keep on doing it throughout our lives and only in cases of certain conditions or mental decline is this process inhibited or terminated. Once this approach to learning is fully understood, a great deal of what follows appears common sense, but it only appears so because we are changing our focus on learning – from learning something to people learning by constructing and transforming their own experiences of everyday living. It is about people learning and not about experiments with dogs, rats and pigeons – although this is not to deny the value of such experiments as part of the process whereby we have come to understand human learning better.

This second chapter has three sections. The first records the research process that I undertook in building the model of learning on which this book is based and it also outlines the different types of learning that were discovered. The second part is about learning in different social situations. The third is about the learning society. Thereafter, the book focuses upon the implications of such an approach to learning for later life.

The processes of learning

Traditionally, learning has been defined in behavioural terms, eg learning is a change in behaviour as a result of experience or practice. This approach reflects the research work with children and in animal psychology. However, it is a very narrow and restricted understanding of learning based on very limited research. The fact that learning is intimately related to action is not disputed, but the definition that I provided at the outset of this chapter and which emanates from my research is much broader. It is, in effect, the process through which human beings develop within their growing and then ageing bodies and continue to do so until they die. It is the moulding of the human essence.

The model of learning which was developed in the research that I am about to describe has been tested and tried in many workshops throughout the world ever since the research was initially undertaken, and it has only been modified slightly. We shall introduce this slightly adapted model later in this chapter. It has also been discussed in many publications (Jarvis, 1987, 1992, 1995, *inter alia*) so that it has been open to testing for a number of years and Merriam and Caffarella (1991, pp 257–58) write that:

> Jarvis's model does deal with learning per se. The thoroughness of his discussion, which concentrates on explaining the responses one can have to an experience, is the strength of the model. These responses encompass multiple types of learning and their different outcomes – a refreshingly comprehensive view of learning. Furthermore, his model situates learning within the social context; learning is an interactive phenomenon, not an isolated internal process.

Their comment on the interactive element of learning is something to which we will return many times in this book. The research itself began as a workshop in which 16 participants were seeking to understand relationships between learning and teaching, so that they could learn how they could best teach adults. First, they had to understand the adults' learning processes. The workshop began with an exercise in which the participants were asked to examine their own learning processes. They were first invited to write down a learning incident in their own lives, to state what started it, how it progressed and, finally, when and why they concluded that it was completed. Having undertaken this exercise they were then paired in order to discuss their different learning experiences. It was suggested to them that they might like to examine the similarities and the differences between them. Significantly, the pairs often discovered that they each had learnt in different ways. Thereafter, two pairs were put together in groups of four and they then discussed their four different learning experiences.

The first time this exercise was conducted the groups were asked to feedback their ideas at this point for a general review. They were asked whether their learning had been skills- or cognitive-orientated, whether it involved a teacher or not, and so on. It became clear from the very first workshop that there were so many differences between them that any single approach to learning would over-simplify the complex processes that they were describing. Thereafter, they were given a simplified copy of Kolb's (1984) learning cycle (see Figure 2.1 below) and it was suggested to them that they might like to adapt it to relate to their own learning experiences.

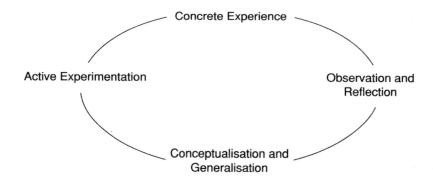

Figure 2.1   Kolb's learning cycle

The participants were informed that the cycle was not necessarily correct and that they were free to adapt it, in any way that they wished, in order to make it reflect their own four experiences. From the feedback from the first set of groups four different models emerged, and a more complex model of learning was constructed by combining them. This exercise was repeated a further eight times in the UK and in the United States. The subjects were teachers of adults and teachers of children; university lecturers and adult part-time university students who were teachers of adults in their full-time occupation; younger people and some not so young participants, and both men and women. In all, about 200 people participated in the exercise but the sample was middle class and not tightly controlled. Each time the last phase was adapted and an even more complex model of learning was constructed (see Figure 2.2 below). This was subsequently tested in seminars in the UK, United States and in Denmark over another nine-month period, with approximately another 200 people participating.

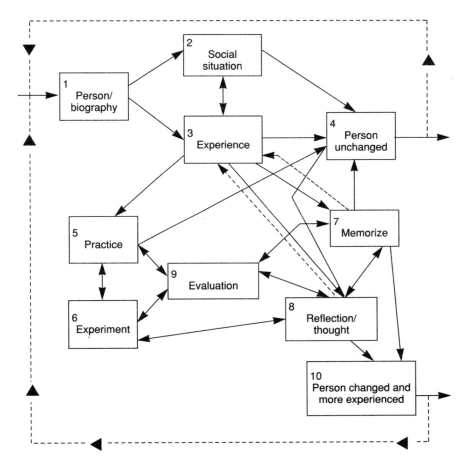

Figure 2.2 The processes of learning

The above diagram looks rather complicated at first glance, and it is. Even so, it is an over-simplification of the complex processes through which we go every time that we learn. The outside dotted line indicates that, whatever the outcomes of our learning experience, it is incorporated into our biographies. At the same time, each of the firm arrows from the outside point beyond the single learning experience to other experiences so that the diagram indicates that time is progressing and other learning experiences may be occurring and also, being built into our biographies. However, we can see that there are four routes out of experience (box 3) – the first goes to box 4. Now this indicates that on occasions we do not learn anything from the experience, for whatever reason, and so we do not grow as a result. But look at the remainder of the routes to:

- box 5 – we practise what we have experienced – we do something;
- box 7 – we memorize what we have experienced – rote learning;
- box 8 – we think and reflect upon what we have experienced – this can result in accepting the knowledge or the procedure with which the learner has been presented or seeking to change it.

The significant thing about this complicated diagram is that there are a variety of routes through it, indicating that there are many forms of learning that we will examine below. These routes are only illustrative of the complex processes which we call learning and they do not include all of them; neither do they make reference to changes that might occur in the brain itself as a result of the experience. It is also important to recognize that not every potential learning situation results in a learning experience. However, it should be noted from the outset that it is the person – the learner – who enters the situation and has an experience from which learning occurs. Learning is about the person as well as the process. It is the person who learns and this is more important than what is learnt; the person's biography is changed as a result of the process – whatever the age of the learner. Figure 2.2 depicts just one set of learning episodes since there can be a number of processes stemming from the same experience and going on simultaneously and this process repeats itself with every potential learning experience throughout the lifespan.

Another important point to which we shall return in the book is that we all learn from our experiences and these occur in social situations; other people are part of the process of creating these experiences in interaction with the learner – teachers, managers, therapists, carers, and so on. Those who work with older adults should understand the intentional and, more significantly, the unintentional learning that occurs as a result of their interactions with them and we shall return to these ideas in the coming chapters.

It may be useful to summarize these different forms of learning and Figure 2.3 depicts these. Each of these different types of learning has at least one route through the learning process, although in some instances there may be a variety of different possibilities.

Each of the reflective forms of learning can have two possible outcomes: conformity or change.

All of these forms of learning can occur simultaneously, and all of the senses can be involved, which demonstrates the complexity of the processes we are discussing. In the following sections, we will briefly describe some of the main routes through the learning diagram associated with the types of learning mentioned above.

Category of Response to Experience	Type of Learning/Non-learning
Non-learning	Presumption Non-consideration Rejection
Non-reflective learning	Preconscious learning Skills learning Memorization
Reflective learning	Contemplation Reflective skills learning Experimental learning

Each of the reflective forms of learning can have two possible outcomes, conformity or change

Figure 2.3   A typology of learning and non-learning

Non-learning

People do not always learn from their experiences. This is why we start with a discussion of three non-learning responses to experience (refer to Figure 2.2):

● presumption (boxes 1 through 4);
● non-consideration (boxes 1 to 2 to 4, or 1 through 4, or 1 through 3 to 8 to 10);
● rejection (boxes 1 through 4, or 1 through 3 to 8 to 10).

Clearly, it is not always possible to map all the routes, and so the paths provided should only be regarded as examples of the learning processes.

Presumption: This is the typical response to everyday experience; we know what to do in the situation – the experience itself is familiar. There is a sense of harmony between the biography and the individual's experience, so that there is no need to change anything – we know precisely what to do. It involves a sense of trust that the world has not changed and therefore that past successful acts can be repeated until such time as the situation does change. This is a situation with which we are all happy and comfortable. While this appears almost thoughtless and mechanical, it is the basis of a great deal of social living. It would be quite intolerable for people to have to consider every word and every act in every social situation before they performed it. Clearly, as we age we gain more experience and, if we limit our life activities, we are likely to have many presumptive responses to similar familiar situations.

Non-consideration: Non-consideration is another response to potential learning experiences that occurs commonly in everyday life. There are two forms. The first is where the person bypasses the situation (boxes 1–2–4) and the second is when the individual is aware of the potential learning that could occur in the situation and then its effect on the actors varies depending on the circumstances. Individuals realize that their biography and their experience are not in harmony and in order to re-establish this sense of equilibrium they have to adapt and learn something new. This disharmony, I have called disjuncture – an ugly word that is employed to reflect this disequilibrium.

However, people do not always respond to a potential learning experience for a variety of reasons. They may be too busy to think about it, may be fearful of the outcome and wish to shut it out of their mind, or they may not be in a position to understand the situation in which they find themselves. Individuals listening to politicians talking on the television often just turn down the sound, or turn it off, because they do not want to learn what the politician is talking about – maybe this is because they are learning not to trust politicians. Thus, while they might recognize the potential for learning from the experience, they may not be able to respond to it. The more they recognize this, but deliberately do not respond, the more they will learn, incidentally, about themselves. They will be changed but still be unable to cope with the situation. Consequently, there are at least two routes through this learning experience: boxes 1 through 4, or boxes 1 through 3 to 8 to 10.

Rejection: Some people have an experience but reject the possibility of learning that could have accompanied the experience. For instance, think of an older person (or a young one) experiencing the complexity of the modern city and exclaiming, 'I don't know what this world is coming to!' Here is a possible learning experience, an experience of the complex modern world, but instead of probing it and seeking to understand it, some individuals reject the possibility. Anybody who looks at the world and says that they will not have any of their opinions or attitudes changed by it rejects the opportunity to learn. Some older people, and the not so old, may not wish to change their understanding of things since their whole identity is based upon it and so they deliberately reject the opportunity to learn new things. One of the most common reasons for this approach is because individuals hold fixed beliefs about 'the truth', they are sure they are right and so nobody can teach them anything more. Rejection may actually serve to confirm them in positions they already hold. In this case, the route in Figure 2.2 is 1 through 3 to 8 to either 4 or 10.

In a sense, then, presumption is different from the other two forms of non-learning because there is no disjuncture. In the first there is no change, but in the other two there is disjuncture and the individual learners might be changed psychologically. In this sense they may have learnt more about themselves incidentally, but there has been no learning that will enable them to respond to the social situation in a different manner. Sociologically, they have generated no change in their social situation, even though they have played their role within it. However, it is increasingly difficult to imagine the same social situations repeating themselves endlessly, for we live in a society of rapid social and technological change. People are always having different experiences and disjuncture is occurring more often, so that people do learn – whether they are aware of it or not.

Non-reflective learning

The three types of learning that constitute non-reflective learning are (refer to Figure 2.2):

- preconscious learning (boxes 1 through 3 to 7 to 4);
- skills learning (boxes 1 through 3 to 5 – maybe to 9 – to 7 to 4 or 10);
- memorization – or rote learning (boxes 1 through 3 to 7 – maybe to 9 to 7 – to 4 or 10).

These are the types of learning that are usually thought of as 'proper' learning. They share the feature that they do not involve reflectivity and so they merely enable the learners to reproduce the social situation in which they find themselves.

Preconscious learning: Preconscious learning is sometimes called *incidental learning*, although preconscious learning and incidental learning are completely different. Incidental learning might well be conscious but its occurrence is still incidental, and is discussed in the next section of this chapter, while preconscious learning occurs at the edge of consciousness or at the periphery of vision. Typically, individuals monitor and memorize their actions, albeit with a low level of consciousness. Drivers, however, are not usually conscious of all the incidents that occur during their trip, but when discussing it with somebody who asks a specific question, they might respond, 'I think I vaguely recall something like that.' If pressed, they might be able to remember something quite specific. They have learnt, but the learning has not necessarily become conscious knowledge. The same phenomenon often occurs when we recall a smell or a taste, and so on.

Preconscious learning is not likely to occur as a result of experiencing in the communicative mode, although it can take place while the two modes of experience are happening simultaneously and the recipient is concentrating on the secondary rather than the primary experience. We shall discuss experience in more detail in the next chapter. For instance, in carrying on conversations, people are not always concentrating on their environment; they may see things out of the 'corner of their eye' or may be 'vaguely aware' that something else is going on. If pressed they might well be able to recall what they had seen in a preconscious manner and then learn from it in a more conscious fashion. The route through this learning in Figure 2.2 is boxes 1 through 3 to 7 to 4.

However, it will be noted that there is a dotted line from memory back to experience and this is because we sometimes have flashbacks and recall things, or we are placed in a situation where we call to consciousness something that has been remembered preconsciously. Then we have a new experience and follow another learning route, and so on, and we will return to this when we examine reminiscence towards the end of this book.

Skills learning: Skills learning is usually associated with such forms of learning as training for a manual occupation or the training for a high level of fitness. But some learning in preparation for a manual occupation is certainly not non–reflective. Thus this term has to be further restricted to the learning of simple, short procedures, such as those that somebody on an assembly line might be taught. These skills are often acquired through imitation and role models. As we age and our physical abilities slow down, we may take a little longer to master skills, or we may actually become more reflective about it.

Skills learning is another form of learning that occurs in the action mode of experience rather than in communicative interaction. There is a significant relationship between skills learning and knowledge: learners might watch a demonstration and claim that they now know how to carry out a task. However, they only know cognitively and indirectly (through memorization) until they have actually performed the task for themselves. The route here in Figure 2.2 is boxes 1 through 3 to 5 – maybe to 9 – to 7 to 4 or 10.

Memorization: Memorization is perhaps the most commonly known form of learning – rote learning. Children learn their mathematical tables, their language vocabularies, and so on. When adults return to higher education, they sometimes feel that this is the most important type of learning expected of them, and so they try to memorize what the instructor has said or what such and such a scholar has written in order to reproduce it in an examination. Older people sometimes appear to regard the words of the medical doctor with the same authority. The authority speaks and every word of wisdom has to be learnt and memorized. There is a sense in this increasingly complex world that we have to trust complex or expert systems because we just do not have the knowledge or skill to respond in any other manner. In precisely the same manner we might learn a smell or a taste, and so on. Memorization can also occur as a result of past successful acts, memories of which are stored away and form the basis of planning for future action. Thus, it also relates to direct action experiences. The routes through Figure 2.2 are boxes 1 through 3 to 7 – maybe to 9 to 7 – to 4 or 10.

The significance of preconscious learning, skills learning, and rote learning in the wider social context becomes clear. They represent a process of social reproduction. Society and its structures remain unquestioned and unaltered. When people learn this way, they are learning to fit into the larger organization or the wider society. They are learning their place, as it were.

Reflective learning

Thus far it has been shown that learning tends to be culturally reproductive, and this has been the main way of defining it. It was suggested that non-reflective learning inevitably reproduces the social structures of society, but this is not true of reflective learning, of which there are again three types (refer to Figure 2.2):

● contemplation (boxes 1 through 3 to 8 – maybe to 9 to 8 [loop can be repeated as many times as necessary] – to 7 to 10);
● reflective skills learning (boxes 1 through 3 to 5 to 6 to 9 [loop can be repeated in either direction as many times as necessary] and then from 6 to 9 to 7 to 10);
● experimental learning (boxes 1 through 3 to 8 to 9 to 6 [loop can be repeated in either direction as many times as necessary] and then from 8 to 9 to 7 to 10).

Contemplation: Contemplation is a common form of learning for which the behaviourist definitions of learning make no allowance, and yet it could be viewed as a very intellectual approach to learning, because it involves pure thought. It is the process of thinking about an experience and reaching a conclusion about it without necessarily referring to the wider social reality. Contemplation (the word, with its religious overtones, was carefully chosen) can involve not only meditation but also the reasoning processes of the philosopher, the activities of the pure mathematician, and even the thought processes of everyday life. This might also describe many learning processes of older people, as they sit and think, or reminisce, about their past experiences. What distinguishes contemplative learning from the process of thinking itself is the fact that the contemplation is focused thinking. With regard to contemplation, the routes in Figure 2.2 are boxes 1 through 3 to 8 – maybe to 9 to 8 (loop can be repeated as many times as necessary) – to 7 to 10.

Reflective skills learning: In an earlier book, (Jarvis, 1987, pp 34–35) I referred to this form of learning as *reflective practice*, but since practice involves knowledge as well as skills I was forced to change it. This is one of the forms of learning that

Schon (1983) had in mind when he pointed out that professionals in practice tend to think on their feet. In the course of responding to unique situations, they often produce new skills. In fact, many skills are learnt in a totally unthinking manner, and so this may be regarded as a more sophisticated approach to learning practical subjects. It involves not only learning a skill but also learning the concepts that undergird the practice. This makes it possible to know why the skill should be performed in a specific way. In addition, older people may learn skills more slowly and during the process they may reflect on which is the best way for them to do it since they are no longer as physically able as they used to be. In this case, the routes in Figure 2.2 are boxes 1 through 3 to 5 to 6 to 9 (loop can be repeated in either direction as many times as necessary) and then from 6 to 9 to 7 to 10.

Experimental learning: In experimental learning, theory is tried out in practice, and the result is a new form of knowledge that captures social reality. This approach to learning demonstrates the way that individuals are always thinking and devising new practical knowledge for themselves in every walk of life. With respect to experimental learning, the routes in Figure 2.2 are 1 through 3 to 8 to 9 to 6 (loop can be repeated in either direction as many times as necessary) and then from 8 to 9 to 7 to 10.

We have noted that these three forms of learning do not always have to be innovative. The fact that the word *learning* can be used to denote both conformist and innovative outcomes seems paradoxical. Learning can result in agreement and conformity or in disagreement and innovation. It is, perhaps, the latter set of outcomes that makes a consideration of power crucial to any understanding of learning.

The significant thing about all forms of experiential learning is that it can be behavioural, action–based, cognitive, or social. All of these can also occur simultaneously, since experience itself has many dimensions. In other words, this is a much more comprehensive theory of learning. Indeed, it demonstrates many of the points that we made in the opening chapter about the changes that have been occurring in recent years, as society has become late modern, or post-modern. We shall refer to these different forms of learning and non-learning throughout the whole of the book. However, it is clear from this first section that, as a human process, learning is very complex and this model is merely an illustration of how difficult it is to capture this fundamental existential process.

There is one route that we need to note now, to which we referred above and which we shall discuss in later chapters, and that is reminiscence – which takes us from box 7 back to box 3 along the dotted line. Here we have a situation in which our current biography and the situation in which we perceive ourselves to be, act together with our memory to (re)construct a previous experience and from which we may learn afresh through any of the routes that leave box 3. This is a very important form of learning for older people.

The social situation

People rarely learn in isolation and for most of our time we have experiences and learn in different social situations. The people with whom we socialize provide some of the stimulus for what we learn, and even how we learn it. This is often ignored, or forgotten, by people who treat the elderly with abuse etc. It is this to which Kitwood (1997) refers in his excellent humane study of dementia. But these situations vary in many ways. One used quite frequently originated in the work of Coombs and Ahmed (1974) when they discussed formal, non-formal and informal learning situations. At that time they were looking at education and formal referring to school and college settings. For them (Coombs and Ahmed, 1974, p 8), non-formal applied to 'any organized systematic, educational activity carried on outside the framework of the formal system to provide selected types of learning to particular sub-groups of the population, adults as well as children'. At the time they wrote, the idea of education as part of learning was recognized by some scholars – but what they call 'educational activity' we would call a learning activity and, consequently, non-formal applies to any form of systematic learning conducted outside of a formal organization. Informal learning is that form of learning that occurs when a friend or a colleague provides an answer to a problem or shows somebody how to perform a procedure in an informal manner.

Teachers set learning objectives and so on to try to ensure that the students learn what has been decided should be learnt. In other words, our learning is planned for us, or, we might plan it ourselves – in the way that the self-directed learning theorists discuss (see Tough, 1972, Long *et al*, 1998 *inter alia*). But a great deal of our learning is unplanned and incidental. Gehlen (1988) was among the first to highlight this in his anthropological studies. However, Marsick and Watkins (1990) have also emphasized this in their studies of learning in the workplace and we will see its significance with regard to older people in care situations in the later chapters of this study.

We are now in a position to look at the different types of situation in which learning, of all the types we described in the first part of this chapter, can occur (Figure 2.4). In other words, this is an elaboration of box 2 in Figure 2.2.

	Intended	Incidental
Formal	Box A	Box D
Non-formal	Box B	Box E
Informal	Box C	Box F

Figure 2.4 Learning situations

In the above diagram:

- Box A is *formal education and training* in an educational institution.
- Box B can refer to instruction of an ongoing nature that occurs in the work-place, *mentoring*, but it can also refer to the type of learning that goes on in U3A groups when the group is taught – *informal teaching and learning*.
- Box C is *self-directed learning*. It is the type of learning that we undertake when we decide to teach ourselves a computer program, and so on. It can be indi-vidual learning or a group project.
- Box D refers to that *incidental learning* that occurs in formal situations, not always educational, but which the planners of the learning experience did not intend. For example, the realization that the instructor is not really as knowl-edgeable as we thought, or that the room is badly designed, or that the carer does not really treat me as an autonomous individual, and so on.
- Box E also refers to *incidental learning* situations in non-formal learning episodes.
- Box F refers to *everyday learning*, which is probably the most common situa-tion of all, especially in rapidly changing societies. In these we find ourselves in new situations and we have to learn how to cope – by thinking on our feet about our next action, and so on. If we fail to respond to this situation quickly, we usually plan our learning and then the situation moves to box C. However, with older people who have become confused, this next stage does not happen so often.

However, we have to recognize that, as we age, there are often fewer opportuni-ties for formal learning, or even for being taught, but more opportunities for informal and non-formal learning. Additionally, a great deal of our learning is incidental and unplanned at every age. Consequently, it must be understood that this is not specifically a book about educational gerontology – it is a book in which seniors' education forms but one part of a wider understanding of human life – one in which we learn all the time, often incidentally. Lifelong learning is not to be equated with lifelong education. The latter is far narrower than the former.

We shall, naturally, come back to these situations although it is clear that learning in some of them is probably more common to older people than it is to others. However, the social situations in which we find ourselves are part of a wider society and this society has, in recent years, been typified as a learning society. Consequently, the final section of this chapter examines the contested concept of the learning society.

The learning society

The nature of work and communication has changed in recent years. People work with knowledge and the idea of knowledge societies predominates in the countries of Western Europe, the United States and the Asian Pacific (Stehr, 1994). But the term frequently used in these countries is the learning society. Learning can be related to knowledge in two quite distinct ways. The learning is the content of what has been learnt – it is, in this sense, the knowledge. But even more significantly, much of that knowledge is changing with great rapidity, as Lyotard (1984) noted when he suggested that knowledge is narrative, and this demands that the members of those societies continue to learn new information and acquire new knowledge in order to keep abreast with the changes in their society.

However, the learning society is a contested concept and I want to suggest that there are at least four different interpretations that may be placed upon this term, each emphasizing one of its dimensions: futuristic, planned, reflexive and market phenomenon.

The learning society as a futuristic society: When Hutchins (1968, p 133) wrote his classic book on the learning society, he looked to the future and suggested that the learning society 'would be one that, in addition to offering part-time adult education to every man and woman at every stage of grown-up life, had succeeded in transforming its values in such a way that learning, fulfilment, becoming human, had become its aims and all its institutions were directed to this end'.

For Hutchins, education would come into its own and the new learning society would be the fulfilment of Athens, made possible not by slavery but by modern machines. It was the realization of this computer revolution that led Husen (1974) to very similar conclusions. He (1974, p 238) argued that 'educated ability will be democracy's replacement for passed-on social prerogatives'. He recognized that the knowledge explosion would be fostered by a combination of computers and reprographics and he (p 240) foresaw the possibility of 'equal opportunities for all to receive as much education as they are thought capable of absorbing'. Despite Sweden's long history of adult education, Husen still regarded the learning society as being educational and based on an extension of the school system, while Boshier's (1980) book on the learning society in New Zealand started with adult education.

A similar position has been adopted by Ranson (1994, p 106), who has suggested that 'There is a need for the creation of a learning society as the constitutive condition of a new moral and political order. It is only when the values and processes of learning are placed at the centre of the polity that the conditions can be established for all individuals to develop their capacities, and that institutions can respond openly and imaginatively to a period of change.'

Ranson's writing does not cite any of the earlier authors mentioned above, although he approaches the subject from a similar perspective, starting with school education rather than an adult or lifelong education framework. He sees education and learning as ways of producing individuals who will become active citizens in a democratic society. It is futuristic and rather idealistic.

In a sense many of us grew up with this idea that society is getting better, that history has direction and that at some time in the future the good society will appear. In many ways, material conditions are better although this does not mean that we are any closer to the good society, and politicians are still endeavouring to introduce more economic growth and development into society.

The learning society as a planned society: In recent years, governments have been concerned to plan for the learning society, and there have been a multitude of reports, papers and even legislation throughout the world. This is not the place to review all the official reports that have been published on education pointing in the direction of lifelong learning, or indeed of all the reports by commercial and industrial bodies calling for more emphasis to be placed on lifelong learning. That would constitute a book in itself. Nevertheless, there are similar themes running through them all as a result of the significance of the global market – competitiveness, competencies, widening participation, and the need for workers to keep on learning so that countries can maintain their place in the economic world and their people their standard of living. In addition, most of them make some reference to the need for people to learn so that they can grow and develop and participate more in the democratic processes of their society. For instance, the introduction to the OECD report (1996, p 13), states: 'Success in realizing lifelong learning – from early childhood education to active learning retirement – will be an important factor in promoting employment, economic development, democracy and social cohesion in the years ahead.'

In the European Union White Paper (1995, p 18), a similar claim is made: 'The crucial problem of employment in a permanently changing economy compels the education and training system to change. The design of appropriate education and training strategies to address work and employment issues is, therefore, a crucial preoccupation.'

In the British government Green Paper, *The Learning Age*, it is clearly stated that the learning society is something to be created (p 13) and on page 15 that it will be educative in nature:

> In the Learning Age we will need a workforce with imagination and confidence, and the skills required will be diverse: teachers and trainers to help us acquire these skills. All of these occupations... demand different types of knowledge and understanding and the skills to apply them. That is what we mean by skills, and it is through learning – with the help of those who teach us – that we acquire them.

In the foreword to this paper, the Secretary of State does broaden the perspective:

> As well as securing our economic future, learning has a wider contribution. It helps make ours a civilized society, develops the spiritual side of our lives and promotes active citizenship.
>
> (*The Learning Age,* p 7.)

Recognition was paid to older learners when the White Paper, *Learning to Succeed*, was published by the Department for Education and Employment:

> We expect the new Council to work with others to champion lifelong learning, promoting learning to men and women of all ages, including older people as well as returners to the labour market and those with special needs. Older people, for example, benefit greatly from learning. Research has shown that older people who continue to be active learners enjoy healthier lifestyles and maintain independence much longer than those who stop learning. Grandparents can also play an important role in family learning, supporting children to acquire good reading skills.
>
> (*Learning to Succeed*, 1999 para. 7.5.)

Both of these approaches foresee an educative society and as such, it is a phenomenon of which Illich and Verne (1976) were afraid, since they feared people would become imprisoned within a classroom rather than being free to learn from different and less restrictive sources. Indeed, there have even been indications that we need compulsory education for adults, especially the unemployed, and if this occurs then we will need to examine the powers of the state to remove human rights from people. The foundation for the other major approaches to the learning society lies in the fact that the rapid changes that are occurring in society have resulted in the weakening of societal structures and this makes space for individuals to control their own learning.

The learning society as reflexive society: It has been increasingly recognized in recent years that knowledge itself is changing at a very rapid rate, and from this perspective there is a fundamental shift in the conception of knowledge itself – from something that is certain and true to something that is changing and relative. This means that underlying this form of society lies experimentation itself, leading people to reflect constantly upon their situation and the knowledge that they possess to cope with it. Constantly they need to learn new knowledge, but learning new things and acting upon them always contains an element of risk. For risk is inherent in learning but, paradoxically, learning is also a reaction to the risk, of not always knowing how to act in this rapidly changing world. Reflexivity is a feature of modernity (Beck, 1992). Reflective learning is a way of life rather than a discovery made by educators and something to be taught in educational institutions. The learning society is not, then, a hope for the future but an ever-present phenomenon of the contemporary world.

Reflective learning and reflective practice have become commonplace ideas among educators in recent years, echoing the work of Schon (1983). But reflective learning is itself a sign of the times; underlying the approach to society epitomized by Giddens (1990) and Beck's (1992) Risk Society. However, Giddens, and others, have argued that reflexivity is fundamental to the nature of modernity and the speed of change engendered by it, for with its advent modernity overrode tradition of all forms. Giddens (1990, pp 38–39) writes:

> The reflexivity of modern social life consists in the fact that social practices are constantly examined and reformed in the light of incoming information about those very practices, thus constitutively altering their character. We should be clear about the nature of this phenomenon. All forms of social life are partly constituted by actors' knowledge of them. Knowing 'how to go on' in Witgenstein's sense is intrinsic to the conventions which are drawn upon and reproduced in human activity. In all cultures, social practices are routinely altered in the light of ongoing discoveries which feed into them. But only in the era of modernity is the revision of convention radicalized to apply (in principle) to all aspects of human life...

Society has become reflexive and the knowledge that people acquire is no longer certain and established forever – its value lies in its enabling them to live in this rapidly changing society. As society is changing so very rapidly, everybody is required to learn new things in order to keep abreast with everything. This is the unintended informal learning that occurs in everyday life (box F, Figure 2.4), but it is also the situation in which people express their concern that they no longer understand what the world is coming to and so they disengage rather than try to keep abreast. Even so, this tremendous growth in new information and the very rapid changes that are occurring in society reflects the idea that the learning society is intrinsic to modernity.

Indeed, there has been a growth in learning networks, such as the U3A, rather like those learning webs advocated by Illich (1973, pp 75–105), but then he was regarded as radical, although now these ideas are becoming more realistic with the development of the Internet and of all forms of electronic communication. This has led to greater opportunity for those who have the technological knowledge, skill and equipment to access up-to-date knowledge and for those who are knowledge producers to share their ideas and research.

But as some forms of knowledge change more rapidly than others (Scheler, 1980) the process of learning is both individuating and fragmentary to society as a whole. Neither is it something that all individuals desire. They sometimes seek an unchanging world (Jarvis, 1992, pp 206–07), and a harmony with their environment. Endeavouring to discover the certainty of an unchanging world is a reaction to the learning society, as it is to modernity itself, and we will deal with this later in the book.

The learning society as a phenomenon of the market: Contemporary society is also a consumer society and the history of consumerism can be traced back to the eighteenth century (Campbell, 1987). Campbell traces it back to the Romantic period in the eighteenth century, when pleasure became the crucial means of realizing that ideal truth and beauty which imagination had revealed and, significantly, this Romantic movement 'assisted crucially at the birth of modern consumerism' (Campbell, 1987, p 206), so that a longing to enjoy those creations of the mind becomes the basis for consuming new phenomena. In other words, there can be no market economy unless there are consumers who want to purchase the products that are being produced. Advertising plays on imaginary pleasure – and learning becomes fun! Now, as Usher and Edwards (1994) point out, one of the features of contemporary society is that of experiencing – it is a sensate society. This is nothing new, as Campbell has shown, but it is the type of society in which the longings of the imagination can be realized through consumption – so that the basis of advertising is the cultivation of desire.

Whilst learning was equated with education in people's minds, they remembered their unpleasant experiences at school when it was no fun to learn; a barrier to further education was erected and it was one which every adult educator sought to overcome. But once learning became separated from education, then learning could become fun – and there is a sense in which this has become a more popular thing to do in the United Kingdom since the creation of the British Open University. Now people could learn all the things that they had wanted to learn, and they did not have to go to school to do it. They could read books, watch the television, listen to the radio and go and talk with other people – if they wanted. The Open University marketed a commodity, and other organizations have followed. The Open University's foundation marked a crucial step in this process – it moved education of adults away from the school setting and into the consumer society. Now it is possible to learn all the things individuals have wanted to know – by purchasing their own multimedia personal computers and surfing the Web, watching the television learning zone programmes, buying their own 'teach yourself' books and magazines and, even purchasing their own self-directed learning courses. But the providers of these learning materials are now not all educational institutions, and educational institutions are having to change their approach with a great deal of alacrity in order to keep abreast of a market generating information about all aspects of life every minute of the day, so that people have to choose not only what channel they are going to watch but what medium they are going to employ to receive their information! Knowledge production has become an industry, cultivating the desire of people to learn so that they can be regarded as modern.

The learning society has now become a learning market. Significantly, information is a public commodity – contained in every form of media transmission – but learning remains a private activity and knowledge has become personal knowledge (Polanyi, 1962). Herein lies a problem with private learning since one

of the features of the market is that the consumption has to be public – conspic-
uous consumption – and so educational qualifications now become an institutional activity.   Indeed, the certificate is rather like the receipt that the buyer is
given on purchase of a product, and the public education institutions now
accredit learning from prior experience for educational qualifications (Jarvis,
1996) so that people can demonstrate their private learning publicly. But for how
long will they retain their monopoly remains another question. Judging by the
direction of recent events, the answer will be that this monopoly will soon be
broken and education will be but one more provider of information in the
learning market.

Conclusion

Learning, then, is something that occurs in individuals throughout the whole of
their lives. But as this book proceeds we will outline a broad concept of the
learning society in which the health and caring professions have as significant a
role as the educators. The learning process rather than the society in which it
occurs, however, forms the focus of this book.

  Learning involves people changing and adapting to the social situations in
which they find themselves; it is a process whereby their experiences are transformed into knowledge, skills, attitudes, values, beliefs, emotions and the senses. It
involves changes in their biography as they age and develop and it is to this we
now turn.

3

Learning, being and ageing

In the previous chapter we saw how learning is related to the nature of the person and to the individual's experience, and in this and the next chapter we will explore the significance of this relationship. We will demonstrate how learning is an ontological process relating to the broader processes of ageing rather than merely to being educated. Consequently, in this chapter we will explore the ideas of being, ageing and maturing, and in the following chapter we shall look at development and experience, concluding with a discussion about learning from experience.

Being-in-the-world

> Reason, man's blessing, is also his curse; it forces him to cope everlastingly with the task of solving an insoluble dichotomy. Human existence is different in this respect from that of all other organisms; it is in a state of constant and unavoidable disequilibrium. Man's life cannot 'be lived' by repeating the pattern of his species; *he* must live. Man is the only animal that can be *bored*, that can be *discontented*, that can feel evicted from paradise. Man is the only animal for whom his own existence is a problem which he has to solve, and from which he cannot escape. He cannot go back to the prehuman state of harmony with nature, he must proceed to develop his reason until he becomes the master of nature, and of himself.
>
> [Italics in original.] (*Fromm*, 1949, p 40.)

This 'insoluble dichotomy' constitutes the major focus of this chapter since it relates human being and learning; Fromm rightly suggests that humankind has no species patterns, that is, no instincts, and therefore no built-in blueprint for behaviour. It is perhaps this, above all else, that differentiates humankind from the rest of the animal kingdom, because having no instinctual behavioural pattern means that human beings do not necessarily act automatically to be in harmony with the natural environment and, if we are out of phase with our natural, or social, world then we are in, what we called in the last chapter, a state of disjuncture. When we are in this state, we often feel uneasy and we seek to change our behaviour in order to achieve equilibrium again – in other words, we have to learn to adjust to our world. Indeed, this state of disequilibrium is a fundamental cause of learning that is inextricably intertwined with being-in-the-world: it is a part of the human condition. In other words we learn because we do not have instincts. We do talk about doing things instinctively, but we do not have an in-built species pattern of behaviour – the definition of instinct – even though we often like to be able to do things automatically, in harmony with our world.

Humans, however, who have no sense of their physical world, or who are deprived of sense experience from beyond themselves, soon become incoherent and lose their sense of being (Niebuhr, 1984, p 56). Being, therefore, needs always to be in the world and we always need to relate to that social situation in order to be. However, it is this constant endeavour to re-establish harmony with the world that is a significant aspect of this learning process and a major element in this 'insoluble dichotomy' of being-in-the-world. This constitutes the first part of the chapter and we shall return to it later in the book.

Since humankind has no instincts, we are always seeking to achieve harmony with our environment and then, perhaps, its mastery. Consequently, at birth, children do not repeat the patterns of the species but they do have drives that lead them to seek satisfaction for their immediate needs, so that they begin to learn how to satisfy those needs. Human babies have little or no knowledge with which to cope with the world. Indeed, they have not even developed a mind, and it is here that each human story begins. Through interaction, through gesture and communication, children store in their brains the memories that are to constitute their minds. Recently, it has been demonstrated that different types of knowledge are stored in different parts of the brain (see Gardner, 1983). These are the early stages of learning.

George Herbert Mead (Strauss, 1964, pp 158–59) was one of the first to explore these early childhood experiences as part of the process of the development of the self:

> Gestures become significant symbols when they implicitly arouse in an individual making them the same response which they explicitly arouse, or are supposed to arouse, in the other individuals to whom they are addressed. In all conversations of gestures within the social processes... the individual's consciousness of the content and flow of meaning involved depends on his thus taking gestures of the other toward his own gestures...Only in terms of gestures as significant symbols is the existence of mind or intelligence possible; for only in terms of gestures which are significant symbols can thinking – which is simply an internalized or

implicit conversation of the individual with himself by means of such gestures – take place.

Thus from the outset of life and through interactive experiences children begin to store knowledge that enables them to give meaning to their experiences. Initially these interactive experiences are with those who bear and who rear them. Thereafter they are with the wider world. But the mind is the store of memories of the experiences that the children have; it is the biographical basis of each child's self-identity, which emerges and develops as the body of experiences grows.

As a result of interaction with the wider world, the person emerges, both as an identity and as one who has gained sufficient knowledge to cope with the business of living in the world. But if this process is examined a little more carefully, it can be seen that internalizing and memorizing experiences lie at the heart of the process. Children have no instinctual equipment to enable them to cope with the world in an unconscious and taken-for-granted manner, so that they have to internalize and store memories of experiences. From this stock of knowledge, children are able to recognize similar experiences and similar communications. From this store of experiences children are more able to cope with future experiences. In other words, at the very beginning of the construction of the mind, at the start of the emergence of the self, lies the learning process. At first, that process might not be very sophisticated, merely the internalizing of perceptions of gesture and the memory of accompanying acts and then the recognition of the repetition of these acts.

However, it is during the early years of this process that something very profound occurs in the child: the growth and development of mind and self. It is perhaps significant that Luckmann (1967, pp 48–49) wrote:

> Subjective processes of recollection and anticipation are woven into a pattern of memory which contains recollections and anticipations of other individuals. As they become part of such a pattern the subjective processes become stabilized; they partake of an 'objective' reality... are integrated, in the course of social relations, into a determinate and more or less coherent biography for which the individual is held accountable.
>
> These considerations may be summed up as follows. Detachment from immediate experience originates in the confrontation with fellow men in the face-to-face situation. It leads to the individuation of consciousness and permits the construction of interpretative schemes, ultimately, of systems of meaning. Detachment from immediate experience finds its complement in the integration of past, present and future in a socially defined, morally relevant biography.

Thus, for Luckmann, these early learning experiences result in the formation of the mind and the self, and at this time humankind transcends its biological nature and in relationship we realize that which is distinctly human about our existence. Luckmann regards this as a fundamentally religious process, for humans transcend that condition of needing species patterns and develop a mind and then a self. Through learning, individuals develop a moral universe of meaning that becomes the basis for understanding future experience.

There are shades here of the Cartesian argument – I think, therefore I am – and in a sense this is a cognitive experience, which should actually read, 'I think, therefore, I know that I am'. However, it is not the existential one: this starts with existence and so it is necessary to turn the Cartesian truism around the other way and claim that – I am, therefore, I think. Because we are, we are aware of all of these changes, but unless we ourselves choose to change and develop with them then we know that we will rapidly become out of date, and in this lies one of the most profound paradoxes of our existence. Having become a self we continue to learn and we treat the world rather like the animals do with their instinctive behaviour: we seek harmony with the social and physical environment so that we can behave 'instinctively'. The basis of so much everyday behaviour is taken for granted, unproblematic experience, or what we called presumptive non-learning in the previous chapter. It is upon this assumption that behaviour is based, that there is no disjuncture between biography and experience, or as Schutz and Luckmann (1974, p 7) write:

> I trust that the world as it has been known by me up until now will continue further and that consequently the stock of knowledge obtained from my fellow-men and formed from my own experiences will continue to preserve its fundamental validity... From this assumption follows the further and fundamental one: that I can repeat my past successful acts. So long as the structure of the world can be taken to be constant, as long as my previous experience is valid, my ability to operate upon the world in this and that manner remains in principle preserved.

Like the animal with its instinct, this body of learning that has become the mind of each human being can create a harmonious situation with the world, which enables an individual to act in an unthinking manner. Time seems to pass in one continuous stream, unthinkingly behaviour is enacted, and the world is experienced in an almost unconscious manner. The interesting fact about this body of knowledge, this moral universe of meaning, is that it is of a pragmatic nature. It is tested by experience, and for much of the time it works and behaviour can be taken for granted. Being in harmony with the world is a comfortable situation, one in which many people like to be, although 'familiarity does breed contempt'! It might produce boredom, but the paradox is that we still seek this apparently comfortable position. But the type of society in which we live makes this increasingly difficult. This body of knowledge we have is not total, nor is it sufficient for every contingency in the process of living in a changing world. Suddenly an experience is problematic, and for a variety of reasons the store of knowledge is insufficient to cope with the world and so we live in a society where everybody has to learn. There is disjuncture between biography and experience, and this cannot be taken for granted.

This is the experience Fromm referred to as the 'unavoidable disequilibrium' since there are no species patterns of life. But this disequilibrium is a state of being in the world that carries with it uncertainty that is uncomfortable to many people. In order to avoid it, behaviour is habitualized, resulting in social norms for group behaviour and even morals that are legitimated by religions. In modern times this process has been expanded with the rules and regulations of bureaucracy, through the institution of contract and the force of law. Many of these patterns of behaviour can, therefore, be anticipated and the problematics of interpersonal behaviour avoided, but the very creation of such a structure is itself antithetical to the nature of humankind that created it and to the world in which we live. We cannot escape this situation. Disjuncture between biography and experience lies at the beginning of all learning and learning lies at the heart of the processes through which we develop our own humanity.

As we age, however, we take our being for granted and consider the roles that we play more significant. But there are other reasons why our being is significant, for it is in relationship with those who meet our earliest needs that we gain a sense of our own social identity. In part we learn who we are through this interaction. We do not live in this world alone: we need others and others need us. We are with and, in a sense, for other people in the world. As we age, we are used to being with and for others – in the sense of working for family and friends. However, when we age we are still beings with and for others. We are still parents and grandparents and friends – we are still beings in the world. We are, as a present phenomenon, and as we age we learn more about our being and ourselves. Even more significantly, our sense of self is still to some extent dependent on others with whom we learn. Indeed, we are still learning to be ourselves throughout our lives. Our personhood is partially dependent on this – we learn to be the people we are, and this has profound implications as we age and in the next section we shall show how individuals learn and change in a variety of different ways.

Ageing and maturing

In traditional society, learning for the most part was something that occurred almost incidentally. Life was habitualized and people knew precisely what to expect in most situations. Where they could not presume upon that situation, they adopted new behaviours – they did something new, but this was not necessarily regarded as learning. Learning was incidental to behavioural change. Consequently, it is not surprising that early theories of learning were quite behaviourist – nearly all of us know of Pavlov and his dogs and Skinner and his pigeons and rats. Other psychologists, such as the Gestalt school, also worked with animals and looked for the connections between behaviour and thought. Their concern was of the relationship between the stimulus that produced behavioural change and the new behaviour and not really in relating this process to human being.

Now, to a great extent the stasis of traditional society has gone. Society is changing so much more rapidly. In this learning society, we are all struggling to keep abreast with all the changes that are occurring and individuals have become, in part, the authors of our own biographies (Wildemeersch and Jansen, 1992, p 9). They have certain freedoms to make a choice as to what they will experience. At the same time, people do not always have that freedom – they have experiences that they do not choose and, indeed, that they would not choose given the opportunity. However, learning occurs whether we choose our experiences or not. Learning is not so much incidental but experiential. It is, therefore, an actual process of choice whereby events experienced in the world are transformed into the subjective material that nourishes the self and develops it. Learning, therefore, is a crucial bridge between the world and the self, so that the self is not immune from the changes that are happening in the individual's world at any time. It will be noted from the learning diagram (Figure 2.2 in Chapter 2) that as a result of learning or non-learning, individuals are either changed and become more experienced (box 10) or they are unchanged (box 4) if they have not learnt. Learning is the process of creating and transforming experience into knowledge, skills, attitudes, values, beliefs, emotions and the senses, and different scholars have examined different aspects of this process. Here we shall look briefly at the work of Piaget (cognition); Dreyfus and Dreyfus (skills); Kohlberg (values); Fowler (beliefs); and Vaillant (emotions).

Piaget (1929, *inter alia*) showed that the way that we think actually changes as we age – although it might actually be more to do with experience than biological age. For instance, writing in the first half of this century, Piaget concentrated on in-depth studies with small samples of children, which included his own daughter. Herein lies both a strength and a weakness of his work: the strength is that the work is in-depth but the weakness lies in the fact that case studies and small samples cannot be legitimately generalized. Nevertheless, his work has been tremendously influential in school education for many years since; in a series of books, he outlined the way children developed cognitively.

His is a stage theory in which he showed how the way we think changes from being concrete to being abstract as we age, and it is summarized in the following figure, taken from an overview of his work prepared by Jarvis (1972).

Period	Age (in years)	Characteristics
Sensori-motor	0–2	Infant learns to differentiate between self and objects in the external world.
Pre-operational thought	2–4	Child egocentric but classifies objects by single salient features.
Intuitive	4–7	Child thinks in classificatory way but may be unaware of classifications.
Concrete operations	7–11	Child able to use logical operations such as reversibility, classification and serialization.
Formal operations	11–15	Trial steps towards abstract conceptualization occurs.

Figure 3.1 Piaget's stages of cognitive development

Individuals do not develop in isolation, so that it is important to note from the outset the significance of relationship. It is only in relationship with others that we are able to mature, but there is always a tendency to see this process as biologically related – as if we would mature without relationship. Not only is relationship important to our biological survival whilst we are still children, it is crucially important to our moral development.

Apart from these initial criticisms of Piaget's work, there are at least two others: the first that his analysis stops at 15 years of age, whereas individuals continue to grow and to develop cognitively and, secondly, that for him the stages are relatively discrete. The first we will deal with here, the second later when we discuss Kohlberg's work. Some scholars have, for instance, asked what happens beyond the stage of formal operations of thought and Allman (1984, p 75) summarizes some of the answers:

> The results of... Arlin's (1975) study revealed that the ability to ask or discover important questions develops subsequent to the stage of formal operation which results in deriving answers to questions and solutions to problems. Neugarten's (1977) research into middle-aged people's thinking strategies identified an increasing use of reflective thinking. Whereas Moshman's (1979) suggested... the ability to think about one's

own theories and processes of theorizing, also develops subsequent to formal operational thought.

Allman continues with a discussion of Riegel (1979) whose work also points us beyond the formal operational thought mode and he recognized that adults think in dialectical operational thought, which Allman (1984, p 76) describes as 'a type of thinking which results in the discovery of important questions and problems. This demands the abilities to tolerate contradictions and to use the tension between the two or more contradictory explanations as a creative force which allows for the discovery of new questions and problems.'

Thus it may be seen that the main foci of the developmental cognitive theorists after Piaget have been upon reflection and dialectic thought. Riegel (1979, p 365) suggests that: 'an individual at any developmental level may directly progress to its corresponding mode of dialectical operations, reaching thereby a mature level of thinking'. Loevinger (cited Vaillant, 1993, p 328) also follows this line of thought, suggesting that individuals learn to tolerate ambiguity as they develop which, in turn, can lead to creativity (Koestler, 1964). Clearly this is an important development in our thinking about adult learning in recent years, showing how we can hold contradictions in our understanding and learn from them.

Dreyfus and Dreyfus (1980) – cited from Benner (1984) – suggest that we learn skills through a series of progressions as we move from novice to expert – they studied chess players and airline pilots:

- novice – beginners with no experience of the situation in which they are expected to perform;
- advanced beginner – can demonstrate marginally acceptable performance;
- competent – typified by someone who has been doing the job for two or three years;
- proficient – perceives situations as wholes rather than pieces and whose performance is guided by experience;
- expert – has an intuitive grasp of every situation and need not consider a vast range of possibilities.

This is 'practice makes perfect'; over a period of years we learn to do things 'instinctively'. We shall return to this when we discuss everyday life later in the book.

Both Kohlberg and Fowler have produced stage theories that rely on Piaget's initial work, although their stages are neither so discrete nor so specifically age-related. Both have become leading theorists in their own fields of moral and faith development respectively and they illustrate some other aspects of learning from experience.

Kohlberg (1986, p 34–35) proposed six stages of moral development but without reference to age, as Figure 3.2 illustrates. Individuals start from seeking to obey exterior rules and their own interests, and then they become more concerned about pleasing the people with whom they live and participating in a functioning society and, finally, they might develop sufficient moral awareness to be able to choose their own ethical principles.

Level 1 – Pre-conventional

Stage 1 – Heteronomous morality   – sticks to the rule
Stage 2 – Individualism/instrumentalism   – concrete individual interest, aware of other people's interests

Level 2 – Conventional

Stage 3 – Mutual interpersonal   – lives up to other's expectations in order to be seen to be good and can then have self-regard as good
Stage 4 – Social system and conscience   – fulfils social duties in order to keep the social system going

Level 3 – Post-conventional

Stage 5 – Social contract   – upholds relative rules in the interest of impartiality, welfare for all
Stage 6 – Universal ethical principals   – follows self-chosen ethical principles, even when they conflict with laws

(Summarized from Jarvis, 1997, p 57.)

Figure 3.2   Kohlberg's model of moral development

Kohlberg's work illustrates that people's moral development is not entirely age-related and he actually discovered how, at any one time, people's conceptual level contains a mixture of different stages of moral development. Elsewhere Jarvis (1997) has argued that there is only one universal ethical principle at Stage 6 and that is the concern of one person for the other, even though putting the principle into action might have varied outcomes, and we shall return to this in the final chapter of this book.

Fowler (1981), influenced by both Piaget and Kohlberg, devised a similar stage theory for religious faith development. Once more there are six stages, although he adds a pre-stage which he calls infancy, and again not everybody reaches the higher levels of development, although he does suggest ages for the earlier stages.

Once again we see a movement away from the egocentric to the other and then from the other to the ultimate stage of universal compassion. Fowler has been criticized as being specifically Christian in his formulation, although he denies it. Nevertheless, for our purposes, we can see in Figure 3.3 how we can and do develop with experience and age:

Stage 1 – Intuititive–Projective	– egocentric, becoming aware of temporality productive of image formation that will affect later life
Stage 2 – Mythical–Literal	– awareness of the stories and beliefs of the local community which begins to provide coherence for experience
Stage 3 – Synthetic–Conventional	– faith extends beyond family, provides a basis for identity and values
Stage 4 – Individuative–Reflective	– self-identity and world outlook are differentiated, develops explicit system of meaning
Stage 5 – Conjunctive	– faces the paradoxes of experience, begins to develop universals and becoming more other-orientated
Stage 6 – Universalizing	– rarely achieved, totally altruistic and compassionate, a felt sense of the inclusive and ultimate respect of all being

Figure 3.3 Fowler's stages in faith development

Both Kohlberg and Fowler indicate the dialectic approach to learning that we discussed in Riegel's critique of Piaget above. Consequently, we can see from the work of all of these scholars the way that we mature in specific directions as we age and, as we have noted already, it is in relationship that our early learning begins and relationship is central to all of our human being.

Vaillant (1993), a psychiatrist, brings together a number of studies of the significance of relationship and affective bonding in individuals. It is in relationship that we learn to love, identify with and internalize others. Advancements take place in relationship, and in order to learn anything, Vaillant (1993, p 336) says: 'Affective attachment plays a primary role. It is not an intellectual process. Intellect rides on the back of affective bonding. Learning the syntax of mature ego defences is surely as complex as acquiring proper grammar.'

In our cognitive learning we take into our minds the facts, etc, that we learn, but in learning emotions we have to feel for the persons with whom we have interacted and loved. Vaillant suggests that 'we assimilate the people we love by suffusing them with emotion, and taking them inside changes us'. We do this in different ways depending on the way that we cope with the relationship and the situation, and Vaillant (1993, pp 344–53) suggests that there are six processes, often associated with the death of the other:

- incorporation – an absorption of the whole person of the other, whom we mourn, into ourselves, it is associated with pathological mourning;
- introjection – a taking inside of ourselves characteristics of those with whom we have identified;
- imitation – we act like those whom we love;
- internalization – we take the rules and roles of the other into ourselves and make them ours;
- idealization – out of gratitude we assimilate aspects of the person whom we have idealized;
- identification – with the loved one.

Vaillant (1993, p 353) summarizes his position thus: 'incorporation and introjection are ways of believing one *has* the other person. Idealization and identification are ways of being the other person and yet *being* oneself at the same time.' [Italics in original.]

Having looked at some of the possible outcomes of learning we can see how we can transform experience into knowledge, skills, attitudes, emotions, values, beliefs and the senses. We might concentrate on specific areas of interest and grow and develop in some whereas we might not develop so far in others. Nevertheless, there is a sense of continuity, or biography, as the self develops through the learning processes despite all the changes in society. Loevinger (cited Vaillant, 1993, p 328) suggests that 'the most mature "integrated" stage of ego development (is) toleration of ambiguity, reconciliation of inner conflict, and the ability to cherish another's individuality while simultaneously respecting interdependence'. From another perspective, Hudson (1999, pp 130–33) suggests that there are 11 characteristics that occur across the life cycle as people mature:

- The childhood years shape, limit and enrich adult years.
- Healthy adults adapt and grow throughout the adult years.
- The adult years are a process of ongoing change and continuity.
- Social status is a major determinant of adult development issues.
- There are dramatic differences between the styles and priorities of men and women during the adult life cycle.
- Careers and work environments have considerable influence on adult lives.
- Adults in midlife and elderhood often become preoccupied with their mortal limits, death, and time left to live.
- Adults in midlife often experience an increase in individuation and introspection.

- During the adult years, leisure – or, more fundamentally, play – takes on new meaning, as a vehicle for living rather than as a vacation from working.
- A major trend in midlife is the pursuit of personal integrity.
- From midlife onwards, adults frequently become more invested in leadership roles and social contribution.

Some of these points are rather common sense and other overlap with each other, but they do reflect the process of human maturing. We shall also return to some of these points in the coming chapters. But underlying these points lie six core values of adult life, so Hudson (1999, pp 134–36) claims:

- a sense of identity;
- achievement;
- intimacy;
- creativity and play;
- search for meaning;
- compassion and contribution.

Here, then, is one list of values about our humanity and while it is certainly not the only one, it does enable us to see that a great deal of the learning of these values is reflection upon life's experiences – all the reflective forms of learning in the model discussed in the second chapter. But it is also a matter of personal achievement, relationship, knowing and doing and feeling at ease with the world in which we live. It is also a matter of getting the balance right in each of these areas of living. This is part of the process of learning and developing throughout our lives. We have to balance work and leisure when we are in work, but when we are relatively free agents we have to balance things we do for ourselves and things we do for others, and so on. Of course, not everyone grows old gracefully, or achieves that sense of integrity and satisfaction that Hudson suggests. Some people are anguished by their past, others inhibited by it. They carry in their biographies scars that cannot be eradicated – they have learnt hurt, distrust, loneliness and so on. As Erikson (1965, p 260) wrote:

> Although aware of the relativity of all the various lifestyles which have given meaning to human striving, the possessor of integrity is ready to defend the dignity of his own lifestyle against all physical and economic threats. For he [sic] knows that an individual life is the accidental coincidence of but one lifestyle with but one segment of history; and that for him all human integrity stands or falls with the one style of integrity of which he partakes.

Ageing is the process through specific historical time; developing is the process towards a specific goal, towards a certain form of maturity that we desire for our loved ones and ourselves. In bygone ages, our forefathers had little choice in this matter. Erikson was very clear about this dichotomy when he enunciated his life stages, and his concepts are reflected in Hudson's characteristics above.

We can see how people mature and, perhaps, become wiser as they age. We will return to this discussion in the eighth chapter when we examine the wisdom of the elders. Older people can continue to develop in their different ways for as long as they wish, or are able, and then they have to disengage in some ways. We can choose to keep abreast with modern developments or we can opt out and let the world pass us by – but because of the way in which all is change and development, we have no choice but to make a decision. If we do not make one, we have effectively chosen to continue doing what we are currently doing! Whatever our choice, things are changing rapidly so that there will always be disjunction between our biography and our experience of the world, ie we will always keep discovering new things and having new experiences, so that we can never take things for granted and disjuncture is the point from which we begin to learn.

Traditionally, therefore, individuals probably learnt less as they aged because they had seen it all before, and their personal development possibly slowed down. As this coincided with the ageing of their bodies, they were able to review their lives and in passing on their experience to the next generation, they still occupied a useful function in society. They could either experience a sense of well-being and ego–integrity (Erikson, 1965), or they would experience a sense of despair about their life. In a sense, they came to terms with two things, their own past experiences and their present society, and in some way they learnt to live in harmony with them.

Ageing and biography

Learning is, therefore, associated with the way that we age and construct our own biography. It is associated with the way that we perceive our experiences of the world of space and time. There is a beautiful epitaph in Chester Cathedral which sums up the way that many people feel about the passing of time and the way that we age:

> For when I was a babe and wept and slept,
> Time crept;
> When I was a boy and laughed and talked
> Time walked
> Then when the years saw me a man,
> Time ran;
> But as older I grew,
> Time flew.

This epitaph captures a phenomenon with which most people are familiar – our changing selves experiencing time. Time no longer seems static, it appears to be flowing more quickly as every day passes – time speeds up as we age. But the world in which we live in the late twentieth century is also one that has appeared to change more rapidly and we are becoming increasingly aware of transience. Bauman (1992, pp 169–70) epitomizes this experience thus:

> Nothing can be done forever. Knowledge that I studiously master today will become thoroughly inadequate, if not downright ignorance, tomorrow. The skills I learn today by the sweat of my brow will not carry me far in the brave new world of tomorrow's technology. The job I won yesterday in fierce competition will disappear tomorrow. The career whose steps I am carefully negotiating will vanish – the stairs, the staircase, the building and all my prize possessions, my today's pride will tomorrow become yesterday's taste and my embarrassment.

It is, then, not only our experience of a more rapidly passing time as we age; we live in a world in which everything is changing and this seems to get faster with the passing years. We are constantly made aware of the passage of time and the speed of its passing. It is easy to feel that we are not keeping abreast with all the changes, that as we grow older we become obsolete in a world that is being transformed so rapidly.

It is as if the only thing that is unvarying within this sea of change is our sense of self – as being, even though society constructs us differently as we age (see Featherstone and Wernick, 1995). We feel that we are still the same persons in a world that is so different from the one that we knew only a few years before – but that is not true either, for our bodies have aged and we have been transformed and we have learnt and developed. But we still know that it is we ourselves who are alive. Yet as we age, other people tend to treat us differently – they treat us as older persons and, unfortunately, as we become dependent upon others some tend to forget that we are persons at all (Kitwood, 1997). Indeed, Patricia Moore (1999, p 59) tells how she disguised herself as elderly a number of years ago and how she was amazed at how differently she was treated, even by the people whom she knew but who did not penetrate her disguise – we have to learn to be old. But the world in which we live has not always learnt to treat older persons as persons, and even our self-image is abused. We do not have to look far to see it – for instance, when carers call older persons 'dearie', and so on, rather than treat them as genuine human persons.

The world in which we live is open and rapidly changing, whereas previous generations experienced a more slowly changing and more structured society in which many of their experiences of life were determined by social position at birth and so they did not have the opportunity to create their biographies. Hence the child of a farmer became a farmer and son of a merchant became a merchant, etc. Learning was something that occurred early in life; children learnt sufficient to assume their place in society and thereafter when they changed their status in a static society, they went through a 'rite de passage' and learnt their new roles. As individuals grew older in traditional societies, it might have been claimed that they had acquired wisdom since they had learnt from so many previous experiences and that they still had an important function in society. They could pass on their experience to the younger members of their society. But there is a sense in which they did not choose their position in life and to a great extent their learning was of a non-reflective nature as they acquired the traditions of the people. Perhaps through the richness of their lives they added a little to society, almost incidentally, but they were the possessors of society's unwritten knowledge and this was the wisdom that they could transmit to the younger generation.

But consider the current situation. Change is now endemic and people are constantly being faced with a world that is changing. Since the world is constantly new, they may wish to continue to learn about it and to understand the complexities of the world in which they live. Sometimes, however, it is one that they do not understand; they may feel that they have less to pass on to the younger generation and, consequently, they feel less useful. But gradually it is being recognized by some that elders can still play an important role in society, as we saw in the British government's White Paper *Learning to Succeed* in the last chapter. We shall also argue later that there is a considerable role for older people in the workforce.

In traditional society, however, individuals were hardly authors of their own biographies. Few people actually moved from their apparently allotted path in life. Now people are much more the authors of their biographies. In simple terms, biography is the story of a person's life and to read a biography is to read a historical narrative about someone's life, usually that of a famous person. Autobiography is a biography written by the person who is the subject of the narrative. The events that these narratives describe have to be recalled and reconstructed from memories and records of past experiences. They have, however, at some time in the past been present experiences, and it is in this sense of currently constructing biography through the present experiences of everyday life that the concept is used here. Biography refers to the life events of individuals which occur sequentially throughout the lifespan: events which are experienced and from which people might, although not necessarily, learn. It is the later interpretation of these events that constitute the narrative of that person's life.

These events occur through the sequence of time and while some might appear significant when they happen, they might not be adjudged to be so later in life, whilst others might attain greater noteworthiness at a later period. Written biographies tend to pick out the major events of life and discuss these, even when written from an educational perspective (see Houle, 1984, who attempted to highlight patterns of learning by examining a number of notable people). However, it is the historian, the biographer, and even the autobiographer who specifies retrospectively significant and insignificant events in a story of the person's life. By contrast, in the approach to learning adopted here, learning is the process whereby the biography is constructed through every experience of life.

At the same time early retirement is, for many, a time of relatively good health and there is still a considerable period of life expectancy. The changing world presents a new challenge for many but as they get even older, many more prefer to disengage from this world. Havighurst (1970) suggests that these are the last two stages of the lifespan, deciding when to disengage and disengagement. However, it is much more disputable whether this is sequential, or whether it occurs at the ages suggested by Havighurst. For many, life remains a challenge and they adopt a positive attitude towards the world, they keep on developing their own biography since they continue to learn. By contrast, some others do disengage and they want a world that they can understand, one which does not change so quickly and they, therefore, create their own stable social world and seek less risk and rather more security for themselves. In a less changing environment they are confronted with fewer opportunities to learn and to grow, so that their personal development is inhibited in their final years.

Eventually, however, with the process of ageing, the body changes, slows down and becomes less able to do all the things that it could do in earlier days; aches, pains and illnesses become more apparent; often people no longer feel a desire to do the things that they did in their youth. Likewise, they do not always wish to discover new ideas or philosophies. But the world is still changing; it is still a place where there can be danger or security and risk and trust; it is still a place where change presents them with potentially new learning situations; where there are still possibilities of new experiences, new learning and still more personal growth.

But to what end? This now becomes the crucial question. Why keep developing? Why keep learning? Are people entrapped in a world and a life without meaning? One of the other features of modernity is that there is a sense of self-reflection. For much of life there appears to be a threat of personal meaningless because of the world of abstract systems and the powerless of individuals in the face of globalization. Giddens (1991, p 202) suggests that the routinization of daily life often prevents considerations of this for many people: 'The threat of personal meaningless is ordinarily held at bay because routinized activities, in combination with basic trust, sustain ontological security. Potentially disturbing existential questions are diffused by the controlled nature of day-to-day activities within internally referential systems.'

But when the day-to-day activities change and people retire, when the world of work and the routinization of 'busyness' has ceased, then people are still faced with this rapidly changing world of modernity but, also, with a world that no longer obscures the fundamental existential questions. Do they still get involved in the endless round of activities, sustained in a system that somehow avoids the questions of meaning because there are still new experiences to be had and new things to be learnt? Or do they seek to come to terms with their world and discover that, as they uncover one layer of meaning, another is to be discovered underneath, like the layers of an onion (Bohm, 1987)? And, perhaps, discover that there is no end to their quest! Herein lies a crisis within contemporary society, and to which we shall return in the chapter on learning spirituality.

Conclusion

This is the crux of the position adopted in this book – that being aware of all the changes in this late modern world, we know that we have the opportunities to learn and develop and grow as we age but we are also aware that we can opt out of society in some way and slow down, or redirect our biography. This is a paradox of learning, which has been discussed elsewhere (Jarvis, 1992) and to which we will return in a later chapter. But it is recognized here that more than ever before in the history of humankind we have the opportunity to create our own biography through the choices that we make and we recognize that learning is the force through which our biographies develop and expand.

Learning, then, is what makes us who we are. But continuing learning enables us to keep on growing, developing and becoming even more experienced learners and human beings. Jacques Delors (1996) recently chaired a UNESCO committee that produced a report entitled *Learning – the Treasure Within*. But learning is more than a treasure within – it is the process through which we are, and by which we will continue to become, unique human beings at whatever age. However, a great deal of our learning remains our responsibility as we age, although others can initiate experiences that also lead to different ways of knowing.

4

Learning from experience and experienced learners

The last chapter recorded research that shows how we, as persons, develop our cognitions, emotions, skills, understanding of morality and spirituality. But all of this learning comes from our experiences. Indeed, Immanuel Kant (1933, p 30) opened his *Critique of Pure Reason* by claiming that there can be no doubt that all our knowledge begins with experience. Not only those forms of learning that we call 'experiential learning', but *all* learning stems from experience. Learning is an existential phenomenon – because we are, we learn. Learning is the process by which we take our experiences of the world and make them our own, we subjectify the objective world and not only make sense of it but we enable ourselves to function within it. Learning is crucial to our understanding of being. It is the process through which we become ourselves and for so long as our mental capacities remain unimpaired, we are able to continue to learn, grow and develop.

In this chapter, therefore, we will first look at the concept of experience, secondly, discuss learning from experience and, thirdly, we will examine the idea that as we age we become more experienced learners. Finally, we recognize that some of our learning comes from being taught and so we look at teaching more experienced learners. In the first three parts of the chapter we shall discuss experience in the broadest sense, including formal, non-formal and informal situations but in the final section on teaching the situations are more formal.

The concept of experience

Experience is a word with many meanings – a very difficult word to define. It can refer to:

- participation, observation, contact;
- a particular incident;

- the sum total of knowledge and sensations that we have remembered;
- the impact upon a person from an outside phenomenon;
- the actual process of sensing phenomena;
- being moved, feeling.

It should be noted that only the first two of these might be regarded as an experience, whilst the third refers to what we have called in the previous chapter a person's biography. Significantly, this is how Knowles (1980) used the term experience in his discussions of andragogy. However, the final three meanings all refer to the process of experiencing and we explored some of these in the discussion in the last chapter. Moreover, these become more significant in the later chapters of this book when we discuss the unintended learning that goes on amongst older people – how they experience their carers, their surroundings, and so on. Unintended learning is a form of experiencing and is central to our understanding of older people. One of the clearest pieces of research in this field occurs in the feminist literature, on women's ways of knowing. Belenky, *et al* (1986, p 200) found that of all the women they interviewed, nearly all regarded out-of-school experiences as their most powerful learning experiences. However, all three of these types of experience are relevant to the discussions of this book. We have deliberately used the word biography to illustrate the fact that we bring to new experiences the sum total of knowledge and sensations that we have remembered as the framework from which we construct our understanding of new situations and through which we learn from those experiences.

Even so, Oakeshott (1933, p 9) has suggested that the concept of experience is the most difficult one in the philosophical vocabulary to manage. No attempt is made here to enter the philosophical niceties of definition, although it must be recognized that people become more conscious of some events as they occur than they do of others. Individual experience, therefore, refers to the subjective consciousness of current events. As learning begins with experience so some forms of lifelong learning begin with the experiences of ordinary and everyday life. Interestingly enough there are fewer studies on everyday experience than we might expect, although there are a few significant ones to which we can turn as we begin our considerations (Schutz, 1932/1967, Heller, 1984, de Certeau, 1984, *inter alia*).

Everyday life itself is a flow of experience, frequently moving between public and private space, between space that is controlled and that over which there is little or no control. Sometimes that flow of experience appears continuous, which Bergson calls 'duration', when time appears continuous and actions are performed in a taken-for-granted manner. Individuals presume on the world, confident that they can cope with the situation and hardly give a thought to their actions. At other times the flow seems to stop, we have a disjunctural experience, and an action is planned or another reflected on in order to overcome it. Schutz (1967, p 47) writes:

The difference between the flowing experiences in pure duration and the discrete discontinuous images in the space–time world is the difference between two levels of consciousness. In everyday life the Ego, as it acts and thinks, lives on the level of consciousness of the space–time world. Its 'attention to life' prevents its from becoming submerged in the intuition of pure duration. However, if the 'psychic tension' for any reason relaxes, the Ego will discover that what formerly seemed to be separate and sharply defined items are now dissolved into continuous transitions, that fixed images have become supplanted by a coming-to-be and passing-away that has no contours, no boundaries, and no differentiations.

Basically, in pure duration, we immerse ourselves in the process of daily living, presume upon it, and do not differentiate our experiences so that we experience time as a uni-directional, irreversible stream. As long as my whole consciousness remains temporarily uni-directional and irreversible, I am unaware of my own growing older or of any differentiation between present and past. In pure duration we are able to presume upon the situation and our experience, so that we take it for granted and do not learn. As Berger and Luckmann (1966, p 71) write: 'Habitualization carries with it the important psychological gain that choices are narrowed. While in theory there may be hundreds of ways to go about the project ... habitualization narrows these down to one.'

The point about this rather natural process is that it relieves people of having to make decisions and having to learn new things; it enables activity to occur with economy of effort and a minimum of choice. Indeed, once an action has been habitualized, it inhibits further lessons from being learnt because we tend to take recurring situations for granted. This is both a paradox of existence and a paradox of experience and learning. Having learnt that something we know works, we sometimes presume that it will always do so and so we cease to learn from it. Repetition of situations hardly adds to our body of knowledge, etc, and as Heller (1984, pp 175–82) asserts there is a danger of over-generalization or of generalizing from a particular situation. She shows (1984, p 178) that once individuals have over-generalized, there is a tendency for their prejudgements to turn into prejudices: 'In such circumstances, my prejudgements turn into prejudices, which my experience does nothing to correct or overrule, since they are bound up with my interests: that is, I am affectively interested in retaining these prejudices (though not only affectively).'

In these instances it is far harder to get people to change their minds or to learn new things. As we age, clearly we habitualize many of our actions and consequently make prejudgements on many situations which makes it harder to learn. There are times, however, when prejudices appear outmoded or irrelevant and when individuals are forced to recognize that they have to have new experiences. This makes some people defensive and others nervous. Learning is not always an exciting adventure – it is sometimes frightening to people who do not wish to, or cannot, learn new things. For older people (and for some that are not so old) who are in this situation, they either tend to opt out of new situations or they appear inflexible and unchanging. How we respond to these situations depends to some extent on our level of confidence, our willingness to experiment and, even, upon our personality. As we age we develop our own predispositions and so we respond to situations differently. But the fact that we do this means that while there may be a relationship between ageing and the amount of experience that we have, age is not the only factor determining our response.

We do not always habitualize situations and responses to situations are not always prejudged. Often people are forced into new situations and have new experiences – they have a sense of discontinuity, or disjuncture, and may not presume upon their situations: 'The very awareness of the stream of duration presupposes a turning-back against the stream, a special kind of attitude toward that stream, a "reflection".'(Schutz 1967, p 47.)

These disjunctural moments when we turn back against the stream are the times when new knowledge might be learnt, new skills and different attitudes acquired, and new perspectives gained. These are times when individuals learn from:

- new situations and information;
- their past experiences;
- observing the performance of others;
- others' mistakes.

These are the times when we can learn new information and new skills. These are the times when we decide upon a certain form of action or inaction, as the case may be. Throughout our lives, many of these experiences are encountered, incorporated into our biographies; or as Schutz (1967, p 51) claims: 'I live *in* my Acts' and by reflecting upon them – which is outside the process of pure duration and a part of discontinuous time – we acquire meaning.

These subjective events may appear 'real' as they are experienced but the modern world is one in which reality is represented, constructed and even packaged for consumption, so that people have to recognize that what they experience may not necessarily depict the actuality. Indeed, it is rapidly becoming a truism that we live in worlds of other people's making – this is the social construction of reality. Experience can, therefore, be of two types – primary (or direct) and secondary (or indirect). Giddens (1990) refers to the latter as mediated experience, a term that reflects the information society and perhaps the way in which many people experience much of the world. Secondary experience, however, can never occur without primary experience, although the converse is not true and primary *can* occur without the secondary. For instance, we cannot interpret a journalist's understanding of an event that we are watching on television (secondary experience) without some awareness of the room in which we are sitting (primary experience), and so on.

In primary experience, individuals perceive the world directly, they place their own interpretation on it as a result of the biography that they bring to that moment when they are conscious that they cannot take the world for granted, ie they experience disjuncture, their consciousness of the moment is heightened. In secondary experience, they have mediated to them narratives or pictures, or both, which have been constructed by others – the speaker with whom they are inter-acting, the teacher who is explaining some theory, the author/journalist, the film-maker, the editor of the television programme, etc. They may be communicating their interpretation of events that they have experienced or, as Beck (1992) points out, they may be communicating their own non-experience: that is communi-cating things that they themselves have not experienced directly either.

We all make sense of our world as a result of having, and learning from, both forms of experience. But neither gives a totally balanced picture of the world. We all have representations of the reality that we call the world, interpretations of it by others. Giddens (1990, p 7) suggests that two sets of dilemmas exist in the current world: security versus danger and trust versus risk. He writes: 'Modernity, as everyone living in the closing years of the twentieth century can see, is a double-edged phenomenon. The development of modern social institutions and their worldwide spread have created vastly greater opportunities for human beings to enjoy a secure and rewarding existence than any type of pre-modern system. But modernity also has a sombre side, which has become very apparent in the present century.'

It is the two faces of modernity that pose many of the problems: people can feel that they are reasonably affluent and secure in this world and yet the media repre-sent it as being full of all forms of danger – as if it were 'news'. Most people who live in the modern world occupy secure homes unaffected by the ravages of war, rape and even local crime, but it is these things that make the headlines. Most people are aware that, although they feel secure and live in a stable society, they are continually being told that there is always the danger of horrendous war, nuclear disaster, mugging and so on. Danger and risk always appear to be present and their consequences are constantly brought to everybody's attention, even though they may not be their present nor immediate experience – but they learn that they could be!

People are also aware of the wonders of modern science and they know that, although they do not understand all the abstract systems they employ, they can trust them most of the time. Indeed, expert and abstract systems ultimately depend upon the trust of those who use them and the specialized expertise of those who operate them. But, at the same time, there is always the risk that one of the specialist experts may fail to live up to that trust or that the expert system will fail. The other side of the coin of trust and security is risk and danger. Indeed, some people try to lessen their reliance upon a world that they no longer understand

and that they feel is increasingly dangerous and risky, and others opt out of those parts that they no longer trust.

Both primary and secondary experiences are actual experiences and they may not always be separated in people's minds at the time that they occur. Indeed, the secondary experiences invade the mind and frequently appear to take the form of primary experience since it is hardly possible to have a secondary experience without a primary one occurring simultaneously. Nevertheless, individuals may be less conscious of the primary mode of experience when they are having the secondary one. For example, individuals attentively watching a terrifying war scene on the television may be more conscious of that than they are of the taken-for-granted room, but in which they are having a primary experience of sitting. It is, perhaps, for this reason that there has been a move away from the idea of consciousness and a greater focus upon communication in the work of many scholars, such as Habermas. Because people are greatly influenced by their mediated experiences, communication and discourse are significant elements in the study of experience but they do not constitute the whole of it. However, people of all ages may not be critically aware of how their experiences are being constructed by others, so that they may treat reports of phenomena in the same manner as their own perceptions of events, or even place *more* significance upon them since they appear to emanate from a more important source. Although those experiences may or may not reflect accurately the world, they are the conscious and subjective experiences upon which people's learning is based and which sometimes *appear* to reflect that world.

As we saw in the second chapter, the situations from which we learn are more likely to be non-formal or informal and are probably more likely to be unintended than they are to be planned. Consequently, whatever our success or failure at school or college, it is what we learn in life that is going to constitute the main content of the biography. It is the memory of this learning that becomes the interpretative framework that we use to construct our experiences and from which we learn.

Learning from experience

Learning is the process of transforming those experiences of everyday life – but how do we relate biography, situation and experience? This is not, perhaps, quite as simple as it appears and the diagram below (Figure 4.1), which is a slight elaboration on the learning model diagram that appeared in Chapter 2, illustrates this complex process a little more clearly.

But because the world is changing rapidly and we are ageing, our experiences of the physical and social world will frequently be new ones, only some of which will our previous learning have equipped us to deal. Where this is the case, there is a kind of congruence, or harmony, between our biography and our experience and we have no need to learn anything – we can take the experience for granted and act unthinkingly, not even be aware of the passing of time. We often say that we act instinctively on these occasions, although it is not instinct so much as our previous learning. But the content of many of our experiences is not contained in our previous biography, so that we experience disjuncture and have to learn. Late modern society has become a learning society. Heller recognizes (1984, p 199) that all learning begins with the experiences we have in everyday action:

> Action is often followed by review of that action: a reflection or recapit-
> ulation of the action, and distanced from it in time or in time and space.
> (Whether I approve in retrospect of what I have done or not – I think
> about it.) We all know what it feels like to realize after the event what
> we ought to have said or done in the first place – in other words, to have
> hindsight. But inadequacy of preparatory thought is not necessarily to
> blame here: often, action itself produces the feeling that we ought to
> have acted or spoken differently.

If we think back to that model of learning in Chapter 2, we will see how individuals – with all their biographical history – enter the situations of everyday life. As social beings we are aware of the situation and there is a sense in which we construct experiences. We do not perceive situations like cameras taking snapshots of reality. Through our own understanding of the situation, which is itself affected by our own often unconscious psychological history (Vaillant, 1993), we experience a representation of it. This is the construction of our experience.

Indeed, not all experience is necessarily going to result in a great deal of personal maturation since some of the learning that ensues from experience might be merely remembering it, such as being able to recall a place, or a person, or an enjoyable experience they had while travelling, and so on. We might merely remember what we have experienced before and repeat it, or do what we are told to do and do it. These are non–reflective learning processes. Non-reflective learning may provide a biographical basis whereby individuals might enter new situations and presume upon them and not learn, or they may provide a basis for contrasting what they know with new experiences and reflecting upon the differences and learning. It depends how individuals use the memories of their experiences. However, there are times when we plan, monitor and reflect upon our experiences. These we called reflective learning – contemplative, reflective skills and experimental knowledge – and through these we may grow and develop. Consequently, age is not the only factor in the construction of biographical experience. The ability to use our past experiences and learn from them is more significant. Even so, we can see that elderhood might be significant for the manner in which we treat new experiences and also how we use the body of knowledge and skill, and so on, that we have amassed throughout our lives.

Everyday life, then, is a site for everyday learning; the university of life is a reality. We do live in a learning society and our learning is a process of creating and transforming experiences into knowledge, skills, attitudes, values, beliefs, emotions and the senses. It is a process of constructing our own biography, and our own theories about the world. We are basically what we have learnt.

Our experience of the world is a complex phenomenon and we need to consider precisely what it entails. At one level, it is a subjective awareness of a present situation. However, that awareness occurs only in the light of previous experiences; consequently the subjectivity is determined by our past biography: we bring to every new situation our own past, although the extent to which we are always aware of this is a point that Freud's researches have illustrated.

In experiencing, there is a combination of the biographical past with a sensation, or perception, of the present 'external' situation although, on occasions, that 'external situation' can actually be a memory of a previous experience and that occurs during contemplation. Naturally, the sensing or the perceiving is largely determined by our biography and it is, therefore, subjective and individual. Learning is a matter of modifying the individual biography, which in its turn will effect the manner by which future situations are experienced.

Thus it may be seen that the process of experiencing is complex and the above diagram is merely an over-simplification of it. When we enter a situation, we are

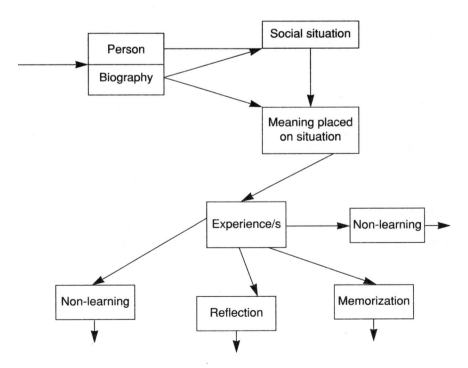

Figure 4.1   The person, meaning and experience

often conscious of the people who are present, their expectations of us, what we feel that we can or should do in the situation, and so on. Often there will be complete harmony between them and we can presume upon it and our experience may hardly be a conscious one. By contrast, if our biography and the situation are not in harmony, what we called disjuncture in Chapter 2, then our experience will be one from which we learn and so we enter the cycles of learning.

This is also a world in which existential questions receive no simple answers. People seek certain and secure answers and find that there might not be any, although groups exist, such as fundamentalist churches, which do provide answers with a degree of certainty that could only have arisen in another age. These answers provide security and some individuals find such an offer attractive and place their trust in them.

This, then, is the world of late modernity into which people are born, live and learn; a sophisticated world of instrumental rationality, but one which presents people with dilemmas that they may not always wish to confront. It is also a world in which people are members of systems and often computer numbers that can be removed at the touch of a button. People themselves appear to be no more than functionaries in a commoditized world. For some, eg Lyotard (1984, 1992), this is a post-modern world with such discontinuities between the past and the contemporary as to suggest that the modernity project has failed and a new era is beginning. The idea of late modernity, by contrast, implies that the consequences of modernity are still being worked out in society but the rate of change has speeded up. Perhaps the reasons for the paradoxes of this age in the West lie in the fact that some countries have high technology and all the aspirations of continued growth, but the idea of a utopian society being created sometime in the future has been destroyed, confidence is being eroded and, as other countries become more competitive, the strength of the West's economies appear to be under threat. This, then, is the world in which people have existential experiences and learn, or otherwise. Learning lies at the heart of this process but, as we have already argued, this is a human process through which we become ourselves. We learn to be us.

More experienced learners

When we are young, our parents and school teachers initiate many of our experiences for us, although children do like to break away from these constraints! However, as we get older we initiate more experiences for ourselves – although whilst we are at work, we are still constrained by the expectations of those who are our managers, employers and so on. As we age, however, we have a greater freedom than ever before to initiate our own experiences and as we showed in the last chapter we have developed a considerable reservoir of knowledge and skills, as a result of our previous experiences in order to assist us in this process. In the final years, other people may initiate our experiences more once again, and we lose some of that autonomy.

Such freedom is paradoxical as I have explored elsewhere (Jarvis, 1992), and to which we shall return later in this book. Experience is also paradoxical, as we saw above, because the more we have the more inclined we are to choose those things with which we are familiar and so deny ourselves the freedom to expand.

In claiming that we become more experienced as we age, I am claiming no more than a truism. Very few great thinkers write their *magnum opus* whilst they are young. They need to become more experienced first – perhaps they need to mature and grow in intelligence. Significantly, Gardner (1983, pp 60–61) in his book *Frames of Mind* suggests that 'a human intellectual competence must entail a set of skills of problem solving – enabling an individual *to resolve genuine problems or difficulties* that he or she encounters and, when appropriate, to create an effective product – and must also entail the potential for *finding or creating problems* – thereby laying the groundwork for the acquisition of new knowledge'.

What he is writing about in his study of multiple intelligences, is a person who is developing more intelligence. In this very significant study he does not, however, refer to another study of intelligence developed by Cattell (1963) and refined by him and Horn in subsequent work – all my references are from Knox (1977, pp 419–23). They developed a theory of fluid and crystallized intelligence. Without going into this in any depth, fluid intelligence is the neurophysiological processes but underlying crystallized intelligence is the process of acculturation – which includes education and active information seeking, and is based on our experiences.

The point of this is that there is a growing acceptance that intelligence is a multi-dimensional phenomenon, or that there is more than one form of intelligence. Cattell's and Horn's work suggests that crystallized intelligence increases with age and experience, and so our more experienced learners are in fact more intelligent people! Being more intelligent, in this sense, depends on retaining our neurophysiological base in good condition, and we shall explore this idea later in this book. The point is, we know that our neurophysiological base declines with age, we lose our physical acuities and research has also shown that our brain changes, but Cattell and Horn argue that since our crystallized intelligence increases more rapidly than the other declines, the sum of the two also usually increases for those actively seeking to learn and grow in intelligence. It is only when we cease to learn – to disengage with culture and society – that the experiential base becomes constrained. Clearly we learn in areas that interest us individually – and provided that we remain mentally healthy there is nothing to prevent us continuing to learn new topics, new subjects and even new skills. This does not make us knowledgeable in all areas, nor does it mean that we will learn other specialisms easily. But neither do younger people necessarily learn them easily. However, it certainly does not mean that we cannot learn them!

We do live in a knowledge-based world where specialist, often technical and technological, knowledge is prized, and since this knowledge is changing rapidly in these specialist areas it takes people who are prepared to limit the area of their learning to specific specialisms to become experts. This, then, is the world of work. It is not surprising, therefore, in this world of rapidly changing specialist knowledge that older people who have not endeavoured to acquire knowledge in one such specialism appear to be out of touch and, perhaps, less intelligent than the specialists. But it might be more true to claim that for those older people who have kept on learning, they are also more intelligent, but in their own areas of specific interest. The theory of multiple intelligences means that we can each acknowledge the other's specialisms without having to claim that one person, or specialism, is more intelligent than another is. Older people may have different interests and concerns and may seek to learn in areas of human life that are beyond the world of work, for instance, in the arts and humanities. At the same time, it has to be noted that older people are seeking to learn how to use the Internet so that they will keep in contact with the wider world and keep on learning.

The third age, therefore, is composed of more experienced learners who might have a greater crystallized intelligence – even learners who are still developing their own intelligence in their own areas of interest. But older people are constantly facing this major dilemma. We are actually free to choose to learn or to leave alone and it is often more difficult to choose to learn than not to learn and it might also require more courage and discipline to learn. All of us are constantly faced with the paradox. When we know that we do not know we need to learn but it might be easier for us not to do so, even though there are things that we know that we would like to learn. It is here that mental discipline enters.

At the same time more experienced learners, and organizations of experienced learners, have some important functions in society. We need to keep on learning to actually develop a wisdom about this world which enables us to embrace it *critically* since this is becoming a risky world and one in which some people find it difficult to oppose authority. Older people have no jobs to lose, etc, and they can engage in the critical debate. Society needs experienced learners who have a disinterested intelligent and critical voice – a voice of democracy – to speak to the wider world.

But it is only through active learning that older people can continue to develop their own intelligence and destroy the stereotype that many people have of older learners. To know that it is possible to keep on learning is not sufficient; it is necessary for people to continue to gain experience and continue to learn.

Older learners being taught

Naturally, older learners are also students, in the sense that some of their learning occurs in formal situations and others in non-formal and informal ones. Many of the new opportunities for older learners occur in fairly formal situations and so it is necessary to recognize that being taught, or teaching, is also part of the experience of most older learners. Older adults do not need to be taught by different teaching methods from younger ones, although teachers of adults at all ages should be very experienced in using the knowledge and skills of their students in their teaching sessions. Opportunity to share experience has always constituted a major element of education for adults, and this is certainly most relevant in teaching older adults. Recognition of the richness of their experience and using it in teaching makes adult learning more exciting, and the teachers are also learners in such situations. However, this is not a book about teaching (see, Jarvis, 1995, and books by Brookfield, 1990, 1995 and Brookfield and Preskill, 1999 *inter alia*), so that the teaching component is not a major one here, although the forms of teaching to which older adults are exposed do help determine their learning in more formal situations.

It has to be recognized that older adults do bring all their biographical experiences to the classroom, and that their experience might include issues being taught and that their experience might be wider than that of the teacher. Consequently, those who teach third age learners do need to be aware of a variety of techniques of teaching – didactic, Socratic and facilitative. But they also need to be aware of the decline in some of the physical acuities, such as hearing and sight and the room must be arranged accordingly, with the right type of equipment – sometimes including microphones and so on.

Didactic techniques, like the lecture, should not be ruled out of third age teaching. Many older adults are used to this method of being taught, and they also expect it. However, they may know a lot of the material that is to be taught, so that it is always useful for the lecturers to check beforehand to discover the level of knowledge of the group. This can be done by asking questions (Socratic techniques) and then agreeing with the group that some lecturing is necessary. However, the concentration span of the learners needs to be recognized, so that lecturers might be wise to break up the lecture with discussion, question and answer and so on, when participants appear to be flagging.

Older learners do have a lot of experience and knowledge; many of them also like to share their experience in a variety of ways, so that teachers might be wise to employ facilitative methods for a great deal of their sessions. Discussion groups are a popular method, but too much discussion tends to get boring and learners do rebel against it. Consequently, varieties of discussion might be used, such as buzz groups, brainstorming and formal debating; group projects might also be undertaken. The significant thing about facilitative teaching is that it allows space for older adults to use their experience and, at the same time, to discover and learn for themselves. In this sense, it is empowering. It enables seniors to take a more active role in society, in their organization or their group, and so on (Cusack, 1999, p 27).

Providing opportunities for older learners to recount their own experience is a useful technique in third age education, since this is another way of providing opportunities for sharing. It is often through sharing that people become empowered and assume responsibility for some of their own activities.

Socratic teaching is the process of the group leader asking questions and seeking to get the learners to think for themselves and develop their own responses. Through this form of teaching, older adults are enabled to demonstrate their knowledge and ability in a way that didacticism prevents.

Many older adults like to do things, to paint, undertake historical projects, and attend physical fitness classes and so on. Age is no bar to activity, even though older people might occasionally act a little more slowly than younger learners. Consequently, teachers of older adults must allow for less rapid reactions to situations than they would get from younger learners – but speed does not always relate to ability!

Many institutions – such as Universities of the Third Age – exist only for older learners, but it should be recognized that many seniors prefer to learn with younger learners. They like to share with them their own experiences but they also want to understand the world of younger people, to join in and learn from it in a variety of different ways. This is not only true of intellectual-type pursuits. Many older people like to attend mixed-age physical fitness classes. Inter-generational learning can be most beneficial to all the learners.

Whilst many of the formal institutions for third age learning conduct classes for which there is no academic accreditation, there are many older adults who still want to study in a formal manner and get academic qualifications for what they do. Indeed, many seek opportunities to study beyond the school-leaving certificate to undergraduate and even post-graduate degree level. Increasingly, opportunities for taught Masters degree study should be a growth area in higher education in the coming years as older people, who have already obtained a first degree and have worked with knowledge for much of their working life, want to pursue formal study in areas of interest in their retirement.

Fundamentally, opportunity for dialogue and exchange of experience is at the heart of a great deal of third age education. The idea that students are also teachers and that teachers are also learners underlies this form of education. Older adults who come to learn in formal situations also have a lot to teach and opportunities for both enrich formal educational classes.

Conclusion

More experienced learners can and do keep on learning but, as we have suggested, many of them will have left work and retired. They have moved through a major transition in their lives and have different interests and concerns. It is, therefore, necessary now to examine the ideas of development, life stages and retirement.

5

Learning to retire

Life may be viewed as a passage through time, but the world in which that journey takes place is undergoing very rapid change. In years past, people could expect to live in a world that changed hardly at all from the time that they were born until the time that they died. They changed and gained more knowledge about it, but the world apparently did not change and so the wisdom of the elders was useful and influential. Elders had lived longer and had learnt the answers to some of the problems that younger people faced. Now things are different. Modernity has brought with it tremendous changes. Whether this is a post-modern phase is debatable, but certainly the world is still undergoing tremendously rapid change and elders are not so highly regarded any more because the knowledge of the modern world is not necessarily *their* knowledge. Apparently it is the knowledge of younger people. This is a period of late modernity.

Living in such a world has implications for older individuals, for their sense of identity and the security that they experience in a world that appears to be constantly changing and unstable. A world of risk, potential chaos and chance. A world where people have to rely on abstract systems and one that seems to be getting smaller as the communication systems alter people's comprehension of space and time. Giddens (1990) talks about space–time distanciation and Harvey (1990) about the compression of space and time. It is a world from which it is easy to feel alienated, especially as we age. We have examined the maturation process in earlier chapters; in this chapter we will explore the process of ageing in terms of stages of life. Thereafter we shall look at one specific transition period – retirement.

The stages of a person's life

Erikson (1965, pp 239–66) was one of the first scholars to discuss life stages and he did so by elaborating on Shakespeare's seven ages of man from *As You Like It*. This he did in his well-known Eight Ages of Man:

- basic trust v basic mistrust;
- autonomy v shame and doubt;
- initiative v guilt;
- industry v inferiority;
- identity v role confusion;
- intimacy v isolation;
- generativity v stagnation;
- ego integrity v despair.

It is only in the final two stages that Erikson focuses upon adulthood, but many of the values discussed by Hudson (1999) in Chapter 3 are developed in the earlier stages of Erikson's typology. We build these into our biographies through learning from experiences in earlier life and carry them with us towards integrity or despair.

Other scholars have looked at the idea that human beings pass through life stages. Perhaps the best known is Daniel Levinson's work on the seasons of life. Initially (1978) he looked at the seasons in a man's life but much later (1996) he looked at the seasons of a woman's life. His idea of seasons was much inspired by the work of van Gennep (1908) on *rites de passage*, but van Gennep's study took place against an entirely different social situation than the one in which we now live. Nevertheless, Levinson's stages and periods of transition can be seen in terms of learning to cope and adapt as we age. I will not recall here the whole of Levinson's typology (1966, p 18) but it can be summarized as:

- pre-adulthood (0–22 years);
- early adulthood (17–45 years);
- middle adulthood (40–65 years);
- late adulthood (60+ years).

It will be noted that between each season Levinson sees a period of transition. This transition period is one in which an individual learns to let go of one set of roles and role behaviours and learns new ones. Perhaps the most obvious area of transition is the midlife transition – that period when we all realize our own mortality and confront the fact, perhaps for the first time. Transitions are periods which anthropologists call liminality, when individuals are learning how to play the new roles attached to their new status in society. However, lifestyles and roles are not really quite so fixed and age-related in late modern society, so that some recent writers have not regarded ageing as a stage developmental process but have merely used biological age as a point in the lifespan to stereotype role behaviour. Both Sheehy (1995) and Hudson (1999), for instance, discuss ageing by 10-year periods, rather than by any more sophisticated theoretical framework. But these are really no more than broad brushstrokes. Giddens (1991, p 148) comments that the lifespan becomes structured around 'open experience thresholds' rather than a ritualized passage. We learn from the experiences we have during life and we develop as we age – but in no particular idealized direction – although there are sets of values and characteristics at which individuals regard it desirable to aim.

One ritual in this process of ageing still remains, but even this is being reconceptualized – retirement. Society still ritualizes retirement and many individuals still undergo such a ritual only once, but some people in this late modern world retire two or three times during their lives. In addition, it used to be something that occurred at a fixed time, eg 65 years, but even this has become variable now. In some careers, eg the military services, individuals retire a lot earlier, but other people are beginning to suggest that 65 years of age is too young to retire since individuals will spend a quarter or even a third of their adult life in retirement. This is costly to the State, in terms of loss of knowledge and expertise and in economic terms too, since the State pays a retirement pension to all who have reached retirement age. Consequently, the State is now beginning to advocate private pension arrangements. Flexi-retirement is being mooted by some as a way of overcoming this situation, with people gradually decreasing the length of their working week. Moody (1998, p 69) notes that there are now the young-old, the old-old and the oldest-old. This latter group is becoming more numerous as the average life span has gradually increased.

We shall examine the retirement ritual here as part of the process of learning to grow old since it is suggested here that when we first undergo this ritual, it does have an effect on our understanding of ourselves as human beings. In addition, it is the first time in some people's lives that they have actually found themselves in this position.

Retirement

It is difficult to determine when later life actually begins. Many apparently older persons will say that they feel quite young and sprightly, whereas some not so old will exclaim that 'they are beginning to feel quite old!' Some people might say that they are old when they reach a specific age, but it is hard to say that people who are 65 years of age are automatically old, if they do not feel old, are still actively employed and still have many activities and hobbies in their private lives. Consequently Moody (1998) asks whether retirement is an obsolete concept now.

So what constitutes later life? Governments might claim that this begins at retirement age, but not all countries have a compulsory retirement age! Indeed, the pensionable age for women has been altered in recent years to create some form of conformity across Europe, and in the United States there is now no compulsory retirement age. These changes have prompted theorists to regard retirement as a way of managing the labour force (Moody, 1998, p 324). Going through the ritual, however, does serve to locate an individual at the edge of the social structure as far as work is concerned. We learn that we have reached a stage in our development and our expectations about what lies beyond may well be mixed. Four dominant modes of experiencing retirement seem to be most prevalent (Gee and Baillie, 1999, p 110, cited from Hornstein and Wapner, 1985):

- transition to old age/rest – relax, slow down and prepare for ageing;
- new beginning – free to tackle long-awaited goals and live life to the full;
- continuity – the basic pattern of life continues;
- imposed disruption – job is irreplaceable and retirement is meaningless and frustrating.

Indeed, Gee and Baillie's (1999, p 126) own research into retirement expectations confirm that there are 'complexities and individual differences in retirement expectations' that present challenges and opportunities. The retirement process is, however, a ritual and so we will now briefly look at the ritual process and then at retirement itself.

In moving from one place to another people often ritualize their moves. They have leaving parties to symbolize that they are about to depart from their present home and after they have moved into a new one they have a house-warming party to celebrate the fact that they have 'put down their roots' in a new abode. (For a full analysis of this, see van Gennep, 1908; Turner, 1974.) This is quite a significant process and has three major parts to it:

- The leaving party is a symbol of departure, which signifies the idea of leaving a place and of breaking the social relationships. It might well be described as a ritual of separation.
- Although there may not be a long period before moving into the new home, there is a short period when a person is in a stage of transition. In the United Kingdom, this might be no more than a day but if a person migrates from one country to another a considerable period of time may elapse before the new home is reached.
- The house-warming party is a symbol of arrival, of putting down new roots and of establishing new relationships. This might be described as an incorporation ritual.

In contemporary society, these parties may hardly appear to be deeply significant rituals, but in primitive societies and in close-knit communities, they had more overtly significant social occasions. Among the functions of the ceremonies are those that signify movement, those that break and create relationships and, above all, that sustain social stability and normality during a transition period.

Because geographical migration in contemporary secular society is such a common phenomenon, its ritualistic significance is not recognized as frequently as it might have been in more primitive societies. Indeed, it might not even be practised. Similarly the rituals that occur as people cross time are less frequently recognized and yet they are still there and new ones are emerging. Travelling through time is a journey upon which everybody embarks from birth. During this journey people occupy different positions in society and different statuses, some of which occur naturally as a result of the ageing process and others because of the level of achievement that individuals reach within the hierarchical structures of society. For example, a person may be a husband and father within the former type of status and managing director within the latter. Each of these statuses is relatively clearly defined and has its own associated roles, and people play those in accordance with their interpretation of the way in which they should be performed.

A much more recent status change has been that of worker to non–worker. In primitive society work was not formalized, nor was it practised far away from the tribe, the village or the family. Work was an integrated part of daily living in the community and something everybody did so that retirement, as such, would not have been understood. It is hardly surprising, therefore, that this status change is not ritualized and enshrined in the religious rites of passage of such societies. It is a new ritual that has developed in our more secular society and so it has not been incorporated into the religious rituals of late modern society. Even so, a secular ritual of retirement has appeared and the process can be examined in precisely the same way as other rituals:

- The ritual of separation might begin at the moment when the company welfare, or training, officer approaches an older person with an invitation to attend a pre-retirement course. Of course, retirement might be a long way off, one or two years in some companies and very occasionally even further. Naturally, this seems important for the company representatives, because it is giving the future retiree the opportunity to consider aspects of life beyond work. But for some employees the invitation comes too early; for them work still has a few years to run and they are not yet ready to think about a future without work. The debate about how long before retirement the company should offer the first day(s) of pre-retirement education is important, but it is not the purpose of this analysis, and therefore it is not pursued here any further. The point is, that this first invitation to attend pre-retirement education might mark the first day in the ritual process of retirement.
- During the following days the potential retirees might well begin to turn their minds to the future, thinking perhaps about some of the issues that have been raised on the pre-retirement course or, even, of others that have been pushed aside in the 'busyness' of everyday life and lain dormant. Additionally, the company might begin to provide cover for these older workers so that their successors can begin to learn the job that they will eventually inherit. This is a period of transition – it might be relatively short or a few years in length depending upon different companies' policies. This period might well end with a last day party, when the company representatives make nice

sounds, present gifts and send the retirees on their way with a good feeling about the company.

- The retirees leave their company and the next stage of the ritual is that of completion of liminality and reincorporation into the wider society.

But this is the problem! Unlike other rituals there is no structural ritual of incorporation. Status change has occurred but in this instance there is no structural or ritual way back into society in order to mark the change and initiate the retirees into their new status and the roles attached to it. Retirement, then, is an incomplete ritual and the incompleteness symbolizes the fact that society has not evolved ways of dealing with retirees in a structural manner, so that they are apparently condemned to always being in liminality. This is what Rosow (1967) called a 'roleless role'. Turner (1974, p 81) describes this period of liminality as a time that is 'neither here nor there... betwixt and between'. At this stage, individuals have a new experience: they are free. Phillipson (1998, p 64), following Atchley (1993) refers to this as emancipation. Provided that the retired have appropriate resources to learn how to be retired people, they are free to create and explore their role how they wish, and to learn from the experiences that they create. They have to devise their own way back into society. However, there is still an expectation that people will 'just wind down and disintegrate' (Goodman, 1999, p 66) after retirement. Our expectations may be one of the problems with which we have to learn to cope when we have retired and are free.

Sheehy (1995, pp 260) describes some of the problems experienced by those who have been forced to take early retirement, rather than those who were able to complete their anticipated working life. She notes their tremendous needs – especially the need to learn how to cope – and how many turn to counselling for help. They have to learn, not only to be, but also to learn new skills so that they can relocate themselves in the world.

If we think back to that model of learning in Chapter 2, people are now free to practise and experiment, free to learn new knowledge and skills, and so on. Retired people have become free agents within society since there are no prescribed structural roles to be played. However, Giddens (1991, p 156), highlights one of the major problems with retirement when he suggests that 'the ontological security which modernity has purchased, on the level of day-to-day routines, depends on the institutional exclusion of social life from fundamental existential issues which raise central moral dilemmas for human beings'. The process of becoming individuated is one that also increases the likelihood of feeling alone. This is an element of the fear of freedom that Fromm (1942) discusses and with which many, including those early-retired people, cannot cope. Now the structures of society do not prescribe role performance and do not shield us from the issues of humanity. Older people are relatively free, perhaps for the first time, to structure their lives in the manner that they wish and to respond to these existential issues in precisely the manner they wish. Herein lies the need to achieve balance – between work and leisure, between self and others, and so on. There are both advantages and disadvantages to freedom – a paradox of human living to which we shall return.

However, being a part of the social structure carries certain privileges as well, and the ritual of separation also removes the retirees from these. Being part of the social structure and having employment provides:

- a sense of personal identity for many people, eg I am a factory manager;
- social identity, eg she is a doctor;
- personal and social worth, eg his work gives him a sense of usefulness to society;
- status and self-respect, eg she has a good position in society;
- a sense of purpose and meaning, eg I can contribute something to society through my work;
- a structure to time, eg for many people the passage of time is structured by the demands of work, etc.

It would be possible to continue with these points and to show that for many people some, or all, of these aspects of their lives are the direct consequence of being within the social structure of society. They also relate to the core values of human development that we discussed earlier in the chapter. When individuals are freed from the structures, they are also parted from all the consequences of being integrated into society. Therefore, at retirement, society ritualizes people out of some, or all, of the consequences of being part of it, but it does not ritualize them back into new structures and consequences, so that it becomes easy for people to be 'lost', and to feel alone in their freedom. We have to learn to be in new roles. Pre-retirement education needs to focus a little more on these key issues.

Pre-retirement education

The first day of a pre-retirement course clearly marks the first day of a ritual that is incomplete and can lead to individuals being ritualized out of society. This is not, therefore, a necessarily desirable state, nor a function of pre-retirement education intended by those who offer this service. Nevertheless, the fact that it is the start of such a process should be recognized by those who are involved in pre-retirement education and they need to be aware of the implications of the freedom.

Mary Davies (1993, p 68) pointed out that traditionally pre-retirement courses were constructed around Heron's formulation that in order to have a good retirement, six factors are necessary:

- good health;
- congenial amicable companions;
- adequate housing;
- adequate incomes;
- something satisfying to do;
- having an adequate personal philosophy.

She suggested that the last of these six receives scant attention — a factor that is quite basic to this book. When I (1980) researched pre-retirement education, I also noted the significance placed on the instrumental aspects of life — health, finance and leisure. Significantly, Gee and Baillie (1999, p 121) note that for both British and Australian retirees, these are still the most dominant topics, although the Australian respondents did specify 'educational courses' as being one of the areas about which they would like more information.

However, this does raise quite significant questions about the design of the learning experiences that should be given to participants in pre-retirement education. Clearly, all participants should be given information and reassurance about these areas of social life in which they are interested. Indeed, early research on pre-retirement education (Phillipson and Strang, 1983, p 202) suggests that reassurance was a major function of the courses that they studied, but the authors also warned educators that some courses actually create more concern in the retirees, and that this is something they need to be aware of. They also recognized the unfinished nature of the retirement ritual and recommended that pre-retirement courses should help to build links between the retirees and the local community (Phillipson and Strang, 1983, p 210).

But there are other aspects of which the participants may not be aware nor have considered for their own lives. For instance, are they aware of the positive functions of work for their own lives that may have to be replaced when they retire? I have conducted courses now for many years and few groups have focused on the significance of personal and social identity. Few have examined the place of work in providing for friendship and the opportunities to make new acquaintances; none have focused on the fact that work has shielded them from ontological issues, and so on. In a session that I have conducted on many such courses, I ask the participants to consider what their occupation provides them in their everyday life that they will lose when they retire, so reducing the quality of their lives. The answers have generally been similar and have included the following:

- an activity;
- finance;
- friendships;
- health;
- identity;
- mental stimulus;

- opportunities to continue learning;
- purpose in life;
- structure of time.

This has normally led to a wide ranging discussion about these topics and how we can find other activities that will replace work. Significantly, however, many of these aspects of everyday living are taken for granted, and it is only when opportunity for careful consideration about life is given, that they are discussed in this way. Few courses, however, have focused on the emotional issues of retirement, although Hepworth (1993) pointed to the significance of a social constructivist approach to emotions in older adults. More recently Goleman (1998, pp 26–27) suggested the following framework for emotional intelligence:

Personal skills
self-awareness – emotional awareness, self-assessment and confidence;
self-regulation – control, trustworthiness, conscientious, adaptable and innovative;
motivation – achievement, commitment, initiative and optimistic.

Social skills
empathy – understanding, developing others, service, leveraging diversity, political;
social skills – influence, communicate, manage conflict, leadership, change catalyst bond-building, collaborative and cooperative, team capabilities.

Importantly, these are the types of human value that Hudson (1999) outlines and which we discussed earlier. They are the skills that help individuals develop themselves and that are especially beneficial in retirement – indeed, they are beneficial throughout the whole of life! Skills like these help potential retirees recognize the structural significance of what is happening to them and help them to become agents to build themselves again and make their own way in society.

   These are significant curriculum issues in pre-retirement education which need to be fully recognized and included within pre-retirement education curricula. However, the fact that there is not a ritual of incorporation remains a fascinating feature of retirement, one to which a number of organizations, religious and otherwise, might turn their attention. But this need not necessarily be a good thing for everybody, since most people go through their lives imprisoned with the structures of society and to be ritualized out of those structures might be a necessary release and a significant step in their own self-discovery and self-development. Yet the freedom gained by some might be a fearful experience for others, and a complete ritual and a structural framework in which to fit their lives may have helped them.

Conclusion

In a sense, retirement is like throwing somebody into the deep end of the swimming pool – they have to learn to swim. But, as we have seen, it is not always easy. Some people will regard it as a new beginning, others as a disruption, others as merely continuing with their lives with a slight change of circumstances and others as a transition to old age. It is, however, a period in which a lot of new learning occurs and it is to this that we now turn.

6

Learning after retirement

In the last chapter we saw how the retirement ritual does not reincorporate retirees into new social roles. After retirement, then, there is a sense of freedom and autonomy that most of us have never experienced before, but there is a sense in which we have to learn what to do with our leisure, even what we can do with our lives. At first sight this might appear easy and even very exciting – but for some, as we saw in the last chapter, it is so difficult that they have to turn to counselling to gain support.

As we have argued throughout this book, learning is a lifelong process (see also Thornton, 1986, pp 62–92). Past experiences should help to prepare people for their present situation: 'Every experience should do something to prepare a person for later experiences of a deeper and more expansive quality. That is the meaning of growth, continuity, reconstruction of experience' (Dewey, 1938, p 47). But not all the experience is an aid to learning, as both Dewey (1938, p 25) and Moody (1986, p 33) point out, and some of our present situations have no previous experiences to guide us. Retirement takes us all into a new realm and most of us have not had past experiences of such freedom, so that while we can rely on much of our past to help us structure our present, we have to learn a lot from our new situations. Hudson (1999, p 180), for instance, notes that when people retire they usually have a rosy picture of what life will be like but they rarely have clear life plans to guide them through the future. In other words, they have undergone a life transition and they now have to learn what it is like to be unemployed and to be autonomous. In a rather strange way, they have to learn what it is like to be free and to control their own time but their future time perspective will have shortened dramatically, so that there may be a tendency to concentrate on the immediate rather than the future. They might also have to learn a new identity and construct some new meanings for life. They will probably also have to learn to structure their lives differently.

In this chapter, we shall explore the ideas of freedom, autonomy and authenticity, then we shall look briefly at learning a new identity and, finally, we shall look at some of the ways that we learn to respond to our freedom. We shall return to the idea about learning the meaning of life in Chapter 8, when we explore it within the context of learning wisdom.

Learning to be free

This is certainly not the place to examine the philosophy of freewill, etc, but it is important to note how our lives are structured by work. Ever since paid occupation was moved from the home environment, the structures of their employment and the demands of their employers have controlled workers. For instance, we even structure time by the structure of the working day – 'it's coffee break time', 'it's nearly knocking off time', and so on. We have to be careful that we do not find too many other pegs on which to structure time when we are free from work, such as, 'it's time for the lunchtime news' and so on. At the same time, if we have no structures and routines, we waste a lot of time dithering around trying to decide what we want to do. Hence, it is not total unstructured freedom that we want, so much as a structured freedom determined by ourselves in relationship with others and something which is sufficiently flexible to allow us to decide to do otherwise on occasions. Yet this is also a problem as we age.

Experience helps to mould us, yet we struggle in a constant effort to understand the changing world. This insoluble dichotomy of human existence asserts itself in old age, for older people have established patterns of behaviour and also systems of meaning that have helped them through the long years of their lives. Hence older people have reached a stage in their development when perhaps it is natural to assume that they can take much of their life for granted, act presumptively, and live in harmony with their world. This might well have been the case when the world changed slowly and people valued the accumulated wisdom of the elders, but that is a world that has since been lost. Now the world changes rapidly, and not only is it not the world into which many of the elderly were born; for some, it is hardly the world into which they retired. There is constant disjuncture between their experience and their biography, and this is both encouraging and disconcerting. A great many experiences in the modern world are potential learning experiences, but many of the past experiences of the elderly may be of little avail in this rapidly changing world. In retirement we have to learn to be free – but the problem is that we might not want to be free or that we fear freedom. Erich Fromm (1942, p 29) aptly summarizes this situation:

> We see that the process of growing human freedom has the same dialectic character that we have noticed in the process of individual growth. On the one hand it is a process of growing strength and integration, mastery of nature, and a growing solidarity with other human beings. But on the other hand this growing individuation means growing isolation, insecurity, and thereby growing doubt concerning

one's role in the universe, the meaning of one's life, and with all that a growing feeling of one's powerlessness and insignificance as an individual.

There is a sense in which retirement cuts the umbilical cord that individuals have established between themselves and the structures of the world of work that has dominated their lives. But the society in which we live still structures a great deal of our lives. Bureaucracy, for instance, has devised standardized procedures and functions most efficiently when people learn these procedures and practise them. Learning within this type of society is, therefore, a non-reflective remembering procedure, and action is a repetition of what has been learnt already. Modern society determines to a considerable extent the type of person necessary to fit into its structures. Consequently, we are never psychologically totally free and we need to create those structures that enable us to function comfortably within the world that we create for ourselves after our first retirement. In this sense, we need to learn to be authentic persons and live authentic lives, so that we continue to grow and develop.

But what, then, is authenticity? Cooper identifies two imperfect models of authenticity. He calls these the Polonian and the Dadaist models (1983, pp 8–25). Polonius said to his son, 'To thine own self be true,' while the Dadaist claims that 'the only requirement for the authenticity of a person's actions and commitments is that these issue from spontaneous choices, unconstrained by convention, opinion, or his own past' (Cooper, 1983, p 10). The former we meet in people of all ages who will not change their minds – they are always acting in character and may be stubborn and inflexible irrespective of the people with whom they are interacting. They are also the people who might be afraid to be free and so, in the freedom of their new world they sustain their own safety imprisoned behind the bars of their own minds. It is these people who might also seek membership of authoritarian-type political and religious groups, which provide them with support structures in an apparently unstructured world.

By contrast, for those with a totally different psychological mind-set, the latter position seems to become more possible after retirement, since these people are less constrained by the structures of society. The Dadaist form of authenticity is to be found in Carl Rogers' writings, which have also been influential in adult education, especially among groups emphasizing human growth and development in their own variety of experiential education. Recognizing that learning does not have to be restricted to education, Rogers (1969, p 295) describes his ideal model of the person who emerges as a result of learning or therapy as follows:

> Here then is my theoretical model of the individual who has experienced optimal psychological growth – the person functioning freely in all the fullness of his organismic potentialities; a person who is dependable in being realistic, self-enhancing, socialized, and appropriate in his

behaviour; a creative person, whose specific formings of behaviour are not easily predictable; a person who is ever changing, ever developing, always discovering himself and the newness in himself in each succeeding moment in time.

This is the Dadaist position: authenticity lies in changing constantly and acting freely and unpredictably. For Rogers, the ideal person is totally free. However, it is questionable whether this is ever actually achieved in society. Even if it were, the question remains whether this is a desirable aim. If the main end of this form of authenticity is for individuals to discover themselves at each moment in time, the end product is a person who is completely self-centred. Indeed, elsewhere, Rogers (1961, pp 163–82) can claim that the aim of life is to be the self that one truly is. It might be asked whether this is really what characterizes an authentic human being. Does the authentic person really act in this self-centred manner? The self is to some extent a product of the social world and constrained by it. People learn during interaction. Do not these types of persons acquire anything from the richness of the people around them? We might ask whether Rogers' ideal person is the type of person we would like to see emerge from the process of living, let alone from education. Even more so, given the opportunities that retirement offers, this is a position that should be avoided.

In an effort to determine the lowest common denominator in these two models of authenticity, Cooper (1983) suggests that both revolve around self-concern. The former implies that human essence precedes existence and so the injunction is to live in accordance with the essential nature of human beings, while the latter emphasizes that what is essential to people is whatever distinguishes them from others, and so people have to be true to themselves. In both of these theories, inauthenticity occurs when individuals are in some way inhibited from expressing themselves.

Other existentialist writers, such as Buber and Marcel, have tended to play down the significance of the individual self and have focused on social interaction as the ideal in human existence. Marcel's (1976) analysis of the interpersonal emphasizes the availability of one person for another. Macquarrie (1973, p 111), in commenting on Marcel's work, suggests that availability means that 'one person is present to another'; that is, people are constantly engaging themselves with others. Buber emphasizes that the fundamental human relationship is not an I–It relationship, but an I–Thou one. He asserts (1961, p 244) that 'the fundamental fact of human existence is neither the individual as such nor the aggregate as such. Each, considered by itself, is a mighty abstraction. The individual is a fact of existence in so far as he steps into a living relationship with individuals. The aggregate is a fact of existence in as far as it is built up of living units of relation. The fundamental fact of human existence is man with man.'

It is only in human interaction that the values society most highly prizes can be manifest. Without interaction, love, truth, peace, justice and so on could not exist. But likewise, there could be no hatred, untruth, injustice and so forth. For these philosophers, authenticity is to be discovered in persons acting in the world and enabling others through relationships to manifest their own personhood. This is a position to which we shall return when we discuss training carers of the elderly, since carers must also allow for the aged and infirm to be persons in the caring relationship. The paradox of the human condition discussed by Fromm may be seen here too: isolated individual existence is not possible, and yet existence with others can only be judged authentic inasmuch as it allows others to become the unique persons that they are. Inauthenticity occurs when relationships are dehumanized, when the individuality and excellence of the other is in some way suppressed, when the richness of human relationships – through which the human being emerges – is in any manner defiled.

Removed from the constraints of work, retired individuals have to work out these relationships and learn to be themselves in this new situation. Few learning theorists have related learning to being in this way, although there are two notable exceptions: Kidd (1973) in adult education and Peters (1966) in initial education. None, as far as I can discover, have done this with older adults who are removed from many of the constraints of work life, with the exception of carers such as Kitwood (1997). Kidd (1973, p 125) argues that being and becoming are both what living is about and that they are also the chief objectives of learning. He discusses learning in terms of the growth and development of the self, recognizing that there is a tension between self-growth and human relationship, which he does not discuss in depth. However, he cites, with approval, Maslow's (1964) study of the lives of people who have achieved both the autonomy of the self and a deep relationship with a few people.

Peters comes close to Kidd and to the ideals of Buber and Marcel when he suggests (1966, p 212) that consciousness of being a person reaches its zenith, perhaps, in the experience of entering into and sustaining personal relationships, which are based on reciprocal agreement, where the bonds that bind people together derive from their own appraisals and choice, not from any status or institutional position. Individuals create their own world by voluntarily sharing together and mingling their own personal perspectives. For Peters, then, a person is a conscious acting being, the highest achievement of which is in coming to terms with the constraints of the world and sustaining personal relationships voluntarily. And this is important in the post-retirement phase of life, when there are fewer institutional structures that bring people together.

We all have to learn to be free in a world that lies beyond work. This is not a matter of non-reflectively accepting the structured world around us, but through reflective learning, through experimentation and practice we have to create our own structures, develop our own relationships and sustain our obligations to others. We have to create our own life world and learn to be ourselves within it.

Learning a new identity

If we are invited to a party, or to drinks, with friends and there are people there whom we do not know, one of our first concerns is to find out what they do, or what they did. It gives us something to talk about. More significantly, it tells us something about the person concerned. Only later are we likely to discover their names. If we are introduced to them, we are often told both. If we have new neighbours move in, we are often more concerned about what they do than who they are. In a real sense, then, we have a number of identities – we have both a personal identity and a social identity, but in many ways the latter plays a more important role in social living. How we perceive ourselves is perhaps more important to us personally.

In pre-retirement classes over the years I have often asked groups to respond to the question, 'Who am I?' (with reference to themselves) by writing down 10 answers. I tell the participants that I will not ask them specific questions about their answers, although I will ask more general ones. The question that I then always ask is – who has put their occupation in the first three answers? Many of the participants affirm that they have done this. Who then are they going to be after they have retired?

We have to learn new identities after retirement – both personal and social – and clearly how we see ourselves is going to play a major role in this. If, for instance, we identified ourselves as beekeepers, then this identity may well be completely unaffected by our change in occupational role. But if we identified ourselves as a company secretary, then our identities would be profoundly affected. Maybe, we would start by saying that we used to be a company secretary – but self-identity by a past role is hardly satisfactory. Recognizing that we can lose one of our main identities at retirement is important – we may have to create new ones, unless we are always trying to refer back to whom we were!

As we noted in the last chapter, our first retirement is significant in this process because the contemporary world emphasizes the significance of work and the fact that to keep abreast in today's world, individuals have to be young, dynamic and abreast with all the rapidly changing technological knowledge. Elderly people just do not have these abilities, so the story goes. By the end of the last century the 'characterization of the aged as "useless", "inefficient", "unattractive", "temperamental", and "senile" accompanied the gradual ousting of the aged from the labour force by the age of 65' (Hareven, 1995, p 131), meant that older people had what Goffman called 'spoiled identities'. Happily, this image is slowly beginning to disappear.

Not all people retire, or change their occupation when they do retire. There is clear evidence that many people just carry on doing the same job, and so reaching retirement age does not mean a great deal to them. There is no reason why people should stop doing what they want to because they reach a certain chronological age. Nevertheless, some people's occupation is not necessarily satisfying for them.

They may want to change their job and learn new roles. This is something to which we shall return in the next chapter. But many may not wish to continue to work and they may seek satisfaction in doing other things. The important thing is that we know what we want to do and what we have to learn to do it. We will then learn new self and social identities.

But we also live in a world where the identities of elderly people are also being created and used in the media and in advertising, and so on. Hearn (1995, pp 107–08), for instance, points out that successful older men are more frequently portrayed on television than older women, and when older men are portrayed the obvious signs of their age – grey hair, paunches etc – are accepted in a manner that is less true of women. Think also of the advertisements on television of contented elderly couples who have invested so wisely in their pension plan, and so forth. Contemporary society is a world of representation and, as Marcus (1992, p 311) notes, one of the significant factors is who or what controls and defines the identity of individuals and groups in today's world. Later in the same paper, he notes how people both resist and accommodate the social pressures by which they are identified. It is like resisting the fact that we are being classified as older people but then having to accommodate ourselves to it. Ylanne–McEwen (1999) records how this process might be conducted through social interaction. In this research, there is an analysis of the discourse of social interaction, when the client of a travel company discusses her requirements for a holiday. Both in the holiday brochures and in the discourse, holidays for older people are the subject of the discourse, and in a rather humorous conversation this perception is negotiated: 'Following the opening encounter – very early on – Mrs Morgan offered a disclosure of chronological age, thus emphasizing age and setting the scene for an inter-generational encounter (with a young female travel agent). She framed the couple's old age as accounting for wishing to travel with older people... At times, then, the identities that were created for the elderly couple as travellers were self-initiated.' (Ylanne–McEwen, 1999, p 436.)

Identity is not something fixed, it is both created and controlled. We have to learn to live with the images of the elderly that are created, even though we might want to be critical of them. Since our own perception of ourselves also affects the way that we play our roles in social interaction, we have to learn to help others see us and treat us in the way that we want them to. This requires a complex process of negotiation with those with whom we interact – but we do have to learn and relearn to be ourselves as older people as we age in a world of images and representations.

Continuing learning

The premise of this book is very straightforward – the elderly can and do continue to learn. Older people also control some of the space in which they live.

Controlling their own lives means that they have opportunities to respond to this rapidly changing world. Not all people will respond in the same manner. Some will find the disjuncture between their biographies and their current experiences too great and they may seek to structure their world in such a way as to reduce this disjuncture, by creating a world with which they experience some harmony. But others may still see the world as a challenge and seek to respond to the disjuncture between their biography and their experience, either actively or intellectually, or both. A number of types of responses to learning may be detected; three common ones are discussed here: those of the sage, the doer and the harmony seeker.

The sages: We are living in a rapidly changing society, one that some scholars regard as post-modern, and others as late modern. Basically, there is a general feeling that the era that began with the Enlightenment is undergoing profound change. New technological and scientific knowledge has meant that the world has become a global village. We are aware of more things about this world than ever before – but we are also only too aware that there is so much that we do not know. The paradox for all of us is that, however knowledgeable we become, the more we realize that there is even more to learn. This is, after all, a learning society and the place of third age learning is growing as we discussed in Chapter 1.

For many older people, the sages, life is still an intellectual adventure. They are still engaged in the quest, still facing the inevitable and unavoidable disequilibrium. They are still content to live without patterns of existence that restrain them. Disjuncture, as always, lies at the start of new learning. But like everybody else in the world, they do not have sufficient interest or time to respond to every potential learning experience. In their later life they do have more freedom to be selective, since they may not be constrained by the demands of employers. They can choose what they want to learn.

As society is changing so rapidly and generating vast volumes of new knowledge, people are aware of how much there is to know. Many opportunities for continuing this intellectual quest now exist. Knowledge is now available in the home through the Internet and other media, educational institutions are realizing that older learners constitute a new market for their learning materials, and specialist institutions for older adults' learning now exist. Indeed, the opportunities for purchasing learning materials and becoming involved in self-directed learning are considerable. Learning to master new subjects and gain knowledge is becoming a common phenomenon. Even so, the opportunity to learn with others is probably even more important. There are now few sections of mainstream education where it would not be possible to find opportunities for older adults to enrol in courses (see Carlton and Soulsby, 1999). Opportunities for learning may be found in:

- adult education institutes;
- further education colleges;
- universities;
- Open University.

In Germany, among other continental European countries, there are also folk high schools that are especially dedicated to older learners, but this has not yet occurred in the UK or United States with respect to formal educational institutions. Indeed, in these institutions older learners may be found enrolled in courses in which younger people are also enrolled. Indeed, many older learners do not want to be separated from other age groups and so they seek out courses that interest them from the general prospectuses of educational institutions. In 1996/97, 11 per cent of all further education funded students were over 50 years of age and 3 per cent were over 60 (Carlton and Soulsby, 1999, p 40). There was, however, a far greater proportion of older student enrolments than this in local government courses, but they were self-funded. The young can gain much from these older learners as older learners can from the young. Yet in a world where the wisdom of the elders is devalued, the learning of this older group is often neglected. Nevertheless, some educational colleges do organize courses especially designed for older people.

In my own personal experience of teaching in adult education for many years, many of the participants have been older adults. Some have wanted to achieve undergraduate – or even postgraduate – qualifications, whilst others have merely wanted to learn for the sake of learning. Overall, universities have been extremely slow to respond to the needs of older learners, despite their long and proud history in extra-mural education (which governments have curtailed in recent years). There has, however been a recent change of heart, as may be seen in the UK government 1999 White Paper *Learning to Succeed.*

Perhaps more significant has been the development of third age learning institutions (discussed in Chapter 1). In the United States, the Institutes of Learning in Retirement emerged in 1962, and by 1972 the first University of the Third Age (U3A) was established in Toulouse in France. Now there are U3As in many countries in the world and an international body (AIUTA – Association International Universities de Troisième Age) which holds a conference every second year with members travelling from all over the world. These universities have different relationships with the more established universities. Crudely there are two main types: the continental model in which European U3As are closely related to their local universities and the UK model where they are voluntary non-governmental organizations. In the former, there is often a more formal teaching and learning role but in the latter there are both formal and non-formal learning opportunities since those who teach may also be members of the same U3A. It is hard to estimate the size of the movement in any one country although there appear to be about 400 separate U3As in the United Kingdom.

Amongst the most popular subjects studied by older people are computer studies, languages, English, music, social sciences, history, arts and crafts, other leisure studies and, even, business studies. Significantly, at least one university in the United Kingdom records the fact that the study of religion and theology is its most popular adult education subject – and this is not surprising amongst older learners. The fact that computing studies is so popular is hardly surprising, as personal computers have become part of everyday life. The University of Ulm in Germany, for instance, has a computer bus that visits various institutions offering older people the opportunity to learn how to use the computer and how to access the Internet. Other forms of distance education, such as the Open University, also offer these opportunities. Opportunities for learning from the Internet are tremendous but it is important to recognize that one of the reasons why older people enrol in educational classes is because they like the personal contact, although this is by no means as significant as interest in the subject.

Chène (1994) showed that community-based learning groups, like the University of the Third Age, fulfil a number of other functions such as providing opportunities to:

● create new friendships;
● generate mutual aid;
● tell stories and share experiences;
● experience a family spirit;
● experience a sense of belonging.

She clearly focuses upon the significance of being with others as something funda-mental to human existence and so the incidental learning is as important, if not more so, than the actual subject being studied. Indeed, Goleman's (1996) study on emotional intelligence also points to the fact that people who are emotionally involved with others enjoy better health and stand a great deal more chance of getting better when they are ill. Thus we can see the importance of being involved with others as we age.

This is a learning society and older learners are a more common phenomenon than ever before in our society. For this group, there is time to be reflective learners, a time to be critical, a time to relate all the new information from the information society to their previous life experiences and a time to grow and develop as human beings (Moody, 1986, pp 122–48). Indeed, there is an emerging body of evidence that suggests that continuing mental activity can help sustain an active brain and delay its deterioration – a point to which we shall return in the final chapters of this book.

The doers: Not all older people want only to be learners, some want to be doers. Consequently, some of them enrol into skills classes in education, such as art and craft, gardening and horticultural classes. However, with the growth of private health and leisure clubs, a growing number of older people are going to the gym, to physical fitness classes and joining in sports for older people. Some of the private physical fitness clubs offer reduced membership fees to older people since they know that seniors are likely to use the facilities at times when other members are at work. Older people are a new clientele for the leisure clubs. Here they learn to be physically fit. There is growing evidence to suggest that such physical exercise, pumping more oxygen to the brain, keeps the brain in a more healthy state. Thus physical fitness might affect mental fitness, a point to which we will return in a later chapter.

A similar philosophy to that of the leisure club applies to the travel industry. With a larger number of older people in good health and tourism a growing industry, more opportunities for cheap travel and cheap holidays now exist. More and more older people are travelling abroad to sunnier climates in out-of-holiday-season times. However, it is not merely holiday travel that is becoming popular. Study holidays are also extremely popular. In the United States, Elderhostel arranges study tours and holidays for thousands of people each year. In the UK, *U3A News* advertises study holidays in its issues. Many adult education institutions and some commercial organizations also offer such opportunities.

Many people can therefore enjoy activity in their retirement – sports, travel, church, societies and clubs, and entertainment. For them, life is still active, and some of their learning is incidental to their doing, although it is still very much part of the process of learning in later life. For some, however, there is a deliberate attempt to combine both – to be learners and doers – and for them, post-retirement life is often more busy than was their work life. It is not rare to hear such people exclaim that they do not know how they found time to go to work before.

Yet, there is another group of doers – those who wish to continue with their work after they have reached the age when they might retire. Hudson (1999, p 180) gives the following advice to those for whom work has been central to their living:

> If work has been a central source of meaning in life up to now, build it into your scenario for your sixties and seventies. It doesn't have to be full-time work or even work in the same career field, but it should be a source of deep meaning and personal fulfilment, not just a way to be busy. Stopping work 'cold turkey' can be a shock to many people who have defined their lives for many many years by their work roles. Just because you are sixty doesn't mean that you *should* stop working. It is up to you. Think it over. [Italics in original.]

Unfortunately, however, continuing to work is often not the decision of the older person. Many employers have mistakenly thought that older people are not as efficient as younger ones, and so on, so that when downsizing has occurred they have automatically dispensed with the services of older people. Some companies have recognized that such a policy is mistaken and have a positive attitude towards employing older people (see Jarvis, *et al*, 1999) and we shall return to this in the next chapter. The Carnegie Inquiry (1993), however, highlighted the often negative stereotypical idea of older people held by employers that disadvantaged both employer and employee. The Carnegie Inquiry (1993, p 27) lists its areas of concern about opportunities for older workers:

- widespread age discrimination;
- frequent compulsion to retire abruptly;
- lack of support in making the transition from full-time work;
- lack of opportunities to re-enter work;
- lack of opportunities for long-term unemployed, leading to abandoning work search;
- available employment is sub-standard, less skilled and lowly paid.

Opportunities for retraining in old age are severely limited, although there are some opportunities in voluntary work (Clennell, 1995), and we shall return to this in the following chapter.

Despite the many recommendations for business to reform itself with respect to older workers, there seem to be few changes and those who have a lot to offer society through their work and to gain personally through their work may still be denied the opportunity to do so to everybody's detriment. Ageism is a prevalent ideology in contemporary society, even in institutions of learning where one would expect to find more enlightened policies.

The harmony seekers: In the model of learning introduced in Chapter 2, it was suggested that a great deal of learning stems from a disjuncture between biography and experience. The discomfort of disjuncture is one of the major motivating factors of learning. Even so, non-learning occurs when people can presume upon their situation and act in a taken-for-granted manner, for when they need not consider the experience or they reject the opportunity so to do. All of us, at some time or another, seek to avoid the discomfort that compels us to learn and so it is not surprising that, as some people age, they seek harmony between their biographies and experiences and reconfirm their previous experiences rather than learn new ones. Harmony seekers are, therefore, those who seek to limit the amount of learning that they undertake in their lives, especially in the latter stages. They may be the old-old or the oldest-old people (see Chapter 5), although, at the time of writing, there is research about learning being undertaken by people who are 100 years old.

Some of the elderly have spent their lifetime seeking to construct a self and a system of meaning that enables them to be at peace with the world and end their days in harmony with it. They represent Erikson's (1965) final stage of life – those seeking integrity. They want mainly to reflect and are happy so doing. But the

world that they have known has passed them by, and they express their amaze-
ment and concern when they ask, 'What is this world coming to?' How do they
respond to this potential learning experience? Do they just keep on learning,
developing mind and a self, in a never-ending quest to achieve harmony with a
world that is constantly changing, or do they recognize that it is a never-ending
quest and that they have to find a harmony in the world they know? If they
cannot presume on the world around them, they can reject the potential learning
experience and even the alien world because they can presume upon it in their
own homes and with other familiar things in their lives. To some extent, they can
shut the world out and live in a world they know. Indeed, they can look back on
the world that has disappeared and can reminisce (Merriam, 1985) and reflect on
experiences long gone but still alive in memory. They can contemplate the past,
even learn from it, but for them, non-learning is essential if they are to hold
together all that has made them what they are. They have developed mind and
the self and now seek harmony and peace. Learning still occurs, but selectively,
and there are an increasing number of instances of presumption and others of
non-consideration or rejection.

Other types of response to learning than these three above no doubt exist, since
these classifications are by no means exclusive, but they do reflect some common
approaches to being and learning among older people and, indeed, among those
who are not so old!

Conclusion

Opportunities for learning after retirement are many, and adult education has
provided advice and guidance about these opportunities. The UK government
has now instituted a national policy on advice and guidance and, while it is clear a
great deal of this relates to vocational education, there are opportunities for advice
and guidance in non-vocational education. It is, therefore, to be hoped that this
point made by Carlton and Soulsby (1999, p 75) is taken note of:

> For older people, the evidence of their involvement in learning in later
> life shows benefits to society, as well as to them as individuals, and yet
> adequate support accessible to all has not been proffered. The new
> national freephone helpline 'Learning Direct' is already dealing with a
> huge volume of calls, and is 'age-blind' in doing so, but it needs a local
> infrastructure of guidance services for more personalized individual
> advice to more older people, targeting those who are less well-informed
> and drawing on voluntary and non-statutory services as well as statutory
> providers.

This chapter has examined the opportunities of learning and doing in post-retirement but it has not yet examined opportunities to learn new roles, although this has been implicit throughout this chapter, and so this is undertaken in the following pages. It is clear, however, that the existence of such a large retired and active population indicates that there is a great deal of under-used social capital in society.

7

Learning new work roles

In the previous chapter we explored the idea of learning after retirement and we highlighted the fact that older learners can also learn to do new things and play new roles. However, there is a philosophy that 'if you do not use it, you lose it' and so we have to be careful in the post-retirement period. Hudson (1999) rightly points out that retirement is not a time when human beings have reached the end of their useful working life and that there will come a time in the future when older workers will launch themselves into new careers. We need to look for new activities that we can do and learn and ensure that we continue to use our faculties. Just as significantly, in the language of contemporary thinking, older people can add greatly to the social capital of a community by the contributions that they make. Social capital is a difficult sociological term for many people to accept since, like a great deal of contemporary capitalist thought, it tends to relate everything people do to the concept of capital rather than to the people who benefit and to the community that is enriched. Nevertheless, in terms of today's thinking, it can also illustrate the fact that older people do have a lot to contribute to society.

Significantly, as this chapter was being redrafted, the British government emphasized its New Deal for people aged over 50 years, which is aimed at those who are unemployed and inactive, in receipt of benefit, for more than six months. This programme comprises employment credit, help with training, personal advice and help in seeking a job. At the time of writing there was no upper age limit to the government's plans, so that the idea of finding new employment later in life no longer seems quite so problematic. Whilst this is still in its early stages of development, it does point to new forms of learning that might become available as the plan unfolds.

In this chapter we will explore a few of the ways in which older people may play new roles, and we will do this in an illustrative way, rather than trying to be exhaustive. Firstly, we will look at the idea of continuing to work after retirement and becoming an informal mentor in the work place. Thereafter we will look at volunteering and, finally, we will examine one especial form of volunteering –

becoming a researcher – since this raises an issue mentioned in the first chapter about playing a role in democratic society.

Continuing to work

We live in a world where youth is praised and older workers are declared redundant. There is a sense that today's managers see only the negative side of older employees and, as one manager responded in our research into companies' attitudes towards older workers – '45 and you're out!' It is almost as if older workers are regarded as obsolescent – that old age is a period of obsolescence or, even more frighteningly, that older people themselves are becoming obsolete. Yet many people do not feel ready to retire or to stop work when they are declared redundant; they wish to continue and some corporations recognize that older workers are reliable, conscientious and responsible. This is true both in the UK and in the United States where Hudson (1999, p 260) writes: 'We live at a time of wasted human assets. Americans have been deluded by the myth of youthism, which is that we decline in all aspects as we get older, particularly after the age of 40 or so. Developmentally this is simply not true, but operationally the myth contributes greatly to the waste of corporate human assets.'

Significantly, however, this is not a battle that is fought at boardroom level. Company directors are not declared redundant at 45 years of age; they continue well into their 60s and 70s. Indeed they are often responsible for some of the problems since they may downsize a company, declare hundreds of workers, often older ones, redundant and then take a large salary increase for apparently making the company more efficient, even if it has caused a lot of people distress. The fact that these older managers and directors feel capable of making rational decisions and working indicates that it is a myth that older people are too old to be employable, but this double standard enables these employers to retire older staff in the name of 'efficiency'. Redundancy may be a way of organizational downsizing and retirement a method of keeping the unemployment levels low, but many people are not ready for full-time retirement at 65 years old. Contemporary protests about the problems of the global market and the recognition that many forms of rationality are actually ideological might just begin to change employer attitudes in the coming years. But there is a greater likelihood that the levels of technology, the demands of global capitalism and demographics will be the overriding factors.

The fact that there is an *Employers Forum on Ageing,* with over 130 members, organized by Age Concern, indicates that this is a problem that some employers have recognized. This forum of employers is seeking to respond to the unpredictable demands of the market and at the same time demonstrate to other UK employers that there are benefits in having an age mix amongst their staff. We shall illustrate this benefit very clearly in the following section on mentoring.

However, it is clear that not all the older potential workforce is in employment and recent research suggests that the decision to take early retirement is much more complex, since expectations of finding further employment plays a significant part in deciding to take retirement in the first place. If there are fewer jobs available, older workers might be less inclined to accept the early retirement package than they were previously. People may seek to continue to work in the same post, unless they are declared redundant, even if they do so on a part-time basis.

Naturally, some people will continue to work in the same job but others will find new careers, sometimes working in the same field that they are already in, but this time working as consultants – using their expertise wherever they can. There are now opportunities to learn how to be a consultant, to be self-employed and to organize a small business. Others will take other jobs (some of which might not utilize their full capacities and where they have less responsibility) but find that they can play a new role in the company. Still others may take on certain forms of voluntary work.

Elders as mentors

Mentoring has become one of the jargon words of modern education and training and it has a variety of connotations. For instance, it has been defined as 'off-line help by one person to another in making significant transition in knowledge, work or thinking' (Megginson and Clutterbuck, 1995, p 13). This definition might be considered too restrictive since it is work-based and implies that any help given by one person to another might actually help make a significant life transition, whereas mentors might play their role many times when there is no such transition. Elsewhere, Clutterbuck (1995, p 4) expanded this definition as he tried to catch something of the broadness and variety of uses of the term, by suggesting that the mentor is a 'long-term guide, counsellor or friend, whose views are valued by the mentee'. However, this restricts the meaning of mentoring to something that is long term and while this might often be the case, it need not always be so.

A slightly more precise definition is that offered by Carmin (1988, cited by Carruthers, 1993, p 10) who suggests that it is 'a complex, interactive process occurring between individuals of differing levels of experience and expertise which incorporates interpersonal or psychological development, career and/or educational development, and socialization functions into the relationship.' This definition does not restrict the relationship to something that occurs outside of the line of management in the way that the first one did, and it also encapsulates the idea of the relationship much better. This is the preferred definition here.

All of the above definitions try to locate mentoring outside of the actual processes of education and training, or human resource development, whereas some professional groups have used the term to refer to specific institutionalized forms of work-based training. These schemes are most often *formalized* and some-times trainers or teacher practitioners are referred to as mentors. Sometimes no distinction is made in these cases between work-based training and mentoring, although there is every possibility that informal mentoring might occur during training sessions.

Mentoring schemes of different types have been established in a variety of orga-nizations, including schools and businesses (Daloz, 1986; Murray, 1991; Caldwell and Carter, 1993; McIntyre, Hagger and Wilkin, 1993; Morton-Cooper and Palmer, 1993; Glover and Mardle, 1995; Megginson and Clutterbuck, 1995; *inter alia*). Indeed, Channel 4 chose mentoring as a topic for its 1995 *Adult Learners' Week* television programmes, and subsequently published a booklet on the topic (Clutterbuck, 1995). Many of these schemes are actually work-based training schemes, which are called mentoring, but our concern is to point to the wider role of the mentor.

Many claims have been made about the success of mentoring and as early as the late 1970s a survey of 1,250 prominent men and women executives in the United States showed that: 'Executives who have a mentor earned more money at a younger age... are happier with their progress and derive greater pleasure from work.' (Murray, 1991, p 18.) Subsequent surveys have suggested that mentoring is a beneficial method of assisting people in the work place. One slightly more measured assessment was: 'Not everyone has made dramatic changes and moved to a new job, but we have noticed a new spirit and an increasing effectiveness among all managers who participated. The work runs more smoothly. We have appreciated the advantages and the profit in backing the mature workers of the staff with time.' (Megginson and Clutterbuck, 1995, p 138.)

Many different occupations, professions and employing organizations are intro-ducing teaching and learning schemes that they call mentoring, even though not all of them are very different from other training schemes that have existed in the past. However, some of these acknowledge the expertise and the wisdom of older workers.

Some employing organizations are also beginning to recognize that not using the knowledge and skill of older people might well be a mistake (Worsley, 1996). One such company, B&Q, is becoming widely known for its positive approach to employing older workers and, indeed, it has found that it can staff its superstores with employees who are 50 years and older as effectively as it can with younger employees. Other companies are also making similar discoveries, so that the normal age of retirement is now not always being enforced by all of them. Older workers have learnt from experience, and they certainly do have a great deal of knowledge and skill. When B&Q decided that it would staff one of its new super-stores completely with over 50s, it was felt that a longer period of preparation would be needed for them before the store opened. In the event, the store opened on time, and it was recognized that 'older employees brought with them a wide range of skills and experience' (Worsley, 1996, p 29).

Elsewhere, Worsley (1996, p 82) points out that when companies employ all age ranges, relationships between the young and the old are often good and that older employees frequently assume 'mentoring roles'. In some research in which I have been involved (Jarvis, Dubelaar and Joyce, 1999), we discovered that in some work-based schemes the older employees were regarded as mentors, even the 'grandparent' in the company who assisted other employees, including their own management, not only with work-based problems but also with personal issues. One employer even has a scheme whereby people wishing to be mentors provide a statement of why they can perform the role and what they can offer and this is made available, in a confidential manner, to employees who wish to have a mentor. Most mentors are older and have a variety of work and personal experiences that they can bring to the mentor–mentee relationship. They were extremely satisfied with their work and felt that they had a considerable contribution to make. Indeed, it is extremely satisfying to mentors to see their mentees gain success, even to go further in their work than the mentors have themselves. Unfortunately, only a few of the corporations with mentoring schemes that use older employees actually offer training for them since they rely more on the life experience of the employees.

These employees have practical knowledge gained through experience, by trial and error and through learning over sustained periods. Nyiri (1988, p 20) maintains that individuals become experts not by acquiring textbook knowledge but by primary experience, trial-and-error experimentation, breaking the rules, and so forth. The experts in the world of work are rather like sages – people who have learnt from their primary experience in a creative manner and are able to act in a repetitive, almost ritualistic, way simply because of the experiences they have had. They are also potential mentors for new recruits to an occupation or profession. They are not seeking to pass on textbook knowledge, although they possess it, but are endeavouring to help the new recruits learn by experience, using their own experiences as guidelines. The wise are experts in living, and the occupational experts are wise in the ways of the world. Both are experts in practical knowledge. While the textbook and the classroom are important in education, education is beginning to rediscover the practical knowledge and wisdom of the experienced practitioner, and the older mentor has become a significant person in preparing new recruits to practice their occupation. Perhaps as managers discover that everything does not necessarily become obsolescent with age, the practical wisdom of the elders will once again play a more significant place in the learning of the young.

Organizations that have introduced mentoring schemes have not necessarily focused upon the older workers as mentors, but on those people who are older than the mentees, or in more senior positions in the management structure. Megginson and Clutterbuck (1995, pp 135–39) record a situation where Svenska Nestlé, in south Sweden, with a staff of 2,300, has a policy called *While the race is running*, the aims of which are '... to let the company's employees of age 45 and over grow as human beings; to give this group a chance to stop for a minute, to think and reflect about their work and their private lives. The project is designed to help those older employees to be motivated and committed to their work, to give them a new spirit and to widen their capacity.'

Significantly, this scheme does differ from the traditional work-based training that is now being called mentoring and the mentors that were chosen for their own executives were external to the company and were around 70 years of age. One of the mentors made the following insightful comment: 'We, who are approaching 70 years of age, have our careers behind us and we do not have to keep our noses to the grindstone. We have the time to commit ourselves to the learners. We also have a vast experience to share with them. Furthermore we do not compete with anyone. We can stay impartial and be fairly objective without letting ourselves be influenced by accidental occurrences or different moods' (p137).

There are other such schemes in which older people are deliberately being employed as mentors to help the young. In Germany, *Old Helps Young* is an organization deliberately established and subsequently supported by the German government, in which older retired executives can be used to support younger people who are just embarking on establishing their own businesses.

It is also clear that mentoring is being encouraged in education and, interestingly, there are inter-generational mentoring schemes in schools where older people are being used as volunteer mentors of children. Schools are discovering that older people are extremely willing to volunteer time to go and work with children, and a number of such schemes have been established in the United Kingdom. As Worsley points out, this also seems to be occurring informally. Schools invite grandparents and local elderly residents to talk to the children about local history, their early lives, and so on.

But it could be asked, why do some older people want to be mentors? Erikson (1963, p 258) discusses the idea of generativity, the primary concern of which is being able to guide the next generation. Also all people need to be needed – a theme also picked up later by Bauman (1992). Consequently, an employer's policy of downsizing and retiring early people of the older age group without careful planning contains a number of fundamental weaknesses and dangers. Such an employer may:

● lose the knowledge and skills learnt throughout the life of the workers;
● lose the potential of people who might both possess the expertise and also have a personal human need to pass on their knowledge and skills to others;
● send out a message to older workers that they are no longer needed.

Significantly, the corporate loss of such expertise might actually be civic society's gain, since many who retire or who take early retirement then enter voluntary work.

Volunteering

Volunteering is becoming important in this new society, which may be an indication of the basis on which a civic society can be reconstructed. Naturally, government is interested in encouraging older people to volunteer for useful services because it is a cheap as well as a worthwhile activity. Many of the jobs that volunteers undertake are not very demanding, indeed rather trivial, and this means that the seniors' abilities are not used to the full. Francis Caro, an American gerontologist, uses the term 'significant volunteering' to refer to the idea that older people should be encouraged to volunteer for demanding jobs that take time, effort and ability. However, Trade Unions have not always supported volunteering since it can be regarded as a cheap form of labour that might be keeping a younger worker out of employment. While this might sometimes be the case, there are instances when non-governmental organizations could not be sustained at all without volunteers. Others claim that volunteering actually enables the government to spend less on the welfare and civic sectors of society, and while this may actually be the case, it is still something that many people find fulfilling.

Gaskin and Smith (1995, p 29), for instance, claim that 25 per cent of people between 55 and 64 and 30 per cent of those 65 and over engage in voluntary activities in the United Kingdom. The higher percentage for the older age group may be a reflection of the need that people who retire at 65 have to continue in socially useful activity. Whether these statistics suggest that a new civic society is emerging, as they claim, is a much more debatable point. What is more certain is that many non-governmental agencies would not be able to exist without volunteers which suggests, at least, that they sustain a major element in civic society. Many countries support the voluntary sector as a vital part of civil society and some are beginning to recognize the significant place that seniors have in it. There are, however, also opportunities for older people to volunteer to work abroad. Indeed, volunteering does bring important benefits to retired people:

> The most important benefit of volunteering is that people simply enjoy doing it. Just over one half of all volunteers [in the Volunteer Centre's survey] said that this benefit is very important. Next in importance is meeting people and making friends and the satisfaction of seeing the results, cited by a third of the volunteers. They also said that volunteering helps them stay active and in good health (29 per cent) and that it broadens their experience of life (24 per cent). Other benefits are experienced by just under one in five of all volunteers. These are the chance to learn new skills, social recognition and a position in the community, upholding or defending their moral, religious or political principles, and the chance to do things that they are good at. Just 2 per cent found none of these benefits very important to them.
>
> (*Gaskin and Smith* 1995, p 49.)

In the Volunteer Centre's survey of eight countries, about 30 per cent of the volunteers received some training and most respondents were satisfied with the training that they received. Opportunities for involvement exist in a variety of social organizations and there is even opportunity to be of service overseas. One agency in the United Kingdom, for instance, is British Executive Service Overseas (BESO) in which retired people, with all forms of expertise, might be placed on its panel of experts. They might then be asked to go on short-term missions to Africa and the poorer Eastern European countries to work with agencies which could not otherwise afford to employ consultants to provide that support and advice.

There is also the increasing employment of older volunteers in schools. Perhaps this is more formalized in the United States than in the United Kingdom and Strom and Strom (1995, pp 322–33) suggest that teachers should identify specific tasks that grandparents might undertake and prepare a volunteer assignment form in which they specify the tasks that they are prepared to entrust to helpers. They also suggest that grandparents should specify their interests on an information sheet and that there should be a screening process before the volunteers are accepted. They also claim that, while grandparents have a lot to offer schools, they also gain themselves: 'Volunteering allows them to help others, remain productive and feel useful... Talking with students promotes new ideas, encourages optimism, and reduces loneliness. The mental stimulation of an academic environment can also improve memory.' (Strom and Strom, 1995, p 329.)

Consequently, it can be seen that volunteering expands life experiences, so that there are many new learning opportunities to be taken simply by assuming a new role after retirement and there are also opportunities to be trained in that role. One more specialized role that some seniors are learning to play, often in a voluntary capacity, is that of researcher.

Older people as researchers

The image of research as being something scientific and far removed from everyday life and the researcher moving in the rarefied stratosphere is gradually being eroded. Research is but another form of learning. One of the mystiques of research has been that it has had to be undertaken using scientific and quantitative methods, entailing large samples, etc, but in more recent times, the exclusivity of this approach has been called into question. Indeed, the validity of the so-called scientific method has itself been open to considerable debate as we have begun to question the values of modernity itself. A new understanding of research has emerged, such as action research (Argyris, Putnam and Smith, 1985), humanistic enquiry (Reason and Rowan, 1981) and practitioner research (Jarvis, 1999). Recognition that research can have validity if it be small scale, localized, participative and even when it has practical outcomes, has changed the nature of research itself. Consequently, it is possible to see that Tough's (1972) understanding of adult learning projects – projects being undertaken for a period of at least seven hours – at least recognizes that adults, even seniors, can undertake the type of learning project that might be conceptualized as research.

Now this does not mean that any haphazard learning can be called research, although the term is sometimes being used rather imprecisely, but it does mean that disciplined, controlled discovery learning is one possible understanding of the concept of research. Research is a systematic investigation of gathering data and interpreting them. In other words, it is a particular approach to learning and close to Tough's understanding of adult learning projects. Adults can be trained to undertake such projects.

Prager (1995) from the Bob Shapell School of Social Work in Tel Aviv describes how 11 volunteers, with an average age of 73 years, were trained in survey interviewing techniques to participate in a pilot study of the frail elderly living in Tel Aviv. Prager (1995, p 216) makes the following point: 'Although the older interviewers may have had more time to record impressions and insights than their younger counterparts had, I could not help but be impressed with the focus and quality of their comments, which revealed their intuitive and experiential understanding of respondents' situations.'

Clearly, then, in this context, the seniors demonstrated that they were insightful researchers. A similar programme has been going on in the United States. At the University of Massachusetts, Boston, the College of Public Service started a Manning Certificate Program in Gerontology which evolved two models of seniors as researchers (Bass and Caro, 1995). In the first, the elders participated in an action research study conducted within the certificate programme itself. The students learnt about the methodology of social research and then participated in an actual research project affecting the elderly. In the second, graduates of the course became interns in a year-long project conducted by the Institute under its Gerontological Social Policy Certificate Program. Bass and Caro (1995, p 475) make the following points, that:

- The elderly actually help the researcher understand the field more fully since they are able to share their experiences.
- As researchers the elderly have often been able to get richer information from older respondents when dealing with open-ended questions.
- The elderly develop informed opinions about policy issues.
- Several older students have been employed by survey research organizations following the course.

Caro (1999) regards the idea of teaching adults applied social research methods, which is providing them with useful knowledge, and then getting them engaged in community projects, as the creation of independent but active citizens' research organizations. He illustrates a number of the projects that have been undertaken in Boston, many of which relate to the institutional ageism that resides in society.

In a similar manner Glanz and Neikrug (unpublished paper) report on a programme at the Bar-Ilan University that has introduced a novel course entitled 'Training Seniors as Researchers in the Study of Aging'. There have been approximately 100 participants in the course and a number of research reports have been published in Israel. The authors conclude that: 'It provides concrete proof to the fact that older people are both capable and competent to carry out research on their social institutions and those of their peers and that they bring to such research work a perspective often absent from the work of young researchers.' (p 3.)

In the United Kingdom the Open University had its own Older Students Research Group – formally recognized by the University as a research group – which undertook a number of European projects, such as looking at the training opportunities for older people working in voluntary work and employment (Clennell 1995). They noted that many older people who are studying with the Open University are also involved in a wide variety of other activities, for some of which they receive training, as we indicated above. In addition, the Pre-Retirement Association started a series of seminars in training seniors in research and this was updated in a seminar at the University of Ulm in Germany in 1995. These were organized and conducted by the authors, Davies and James, and are well attended, indicating that there is considerable interest among seniors in undertaking their own research.

In the research on elder mentoring reported above, some of the interviewers used were volunteers from the local University of the Third Age. It was considered that it was easier for older people to talk with older mentors about what they were doing than to a younger research assistant. More significantly, all three volunteers working as research assistants in this project were experienced interviewers, one was even a trainer, and so little actual training was required for them to fulfil their research role. Indeed, University of the Third Age groups are now beginning to bid for funds to undertake some projects themselves.

There are older individual researchers who undertake projects for awards and for personal satisfaction. John Cunningham, for instance, mapped the range and opportunities available in 50 care homes in Hertfordshire. He was able to see how well-managed homes with a lot of activities generate an air of confidence among their residents, how these activities have to be tailored to the individual home and how it is important to satisfy the physical, intellectual and spiritual needs of each resident (Conference Report – *Carry on Learning*, 1999, p 5).

There is, therefore, considerable evidence that seniors are studying research methods and undertaking research projects on ageing in a variety of different countries. Most of this evidence points to practical-type projects that many universities might regard as low level but, nevertheless, does indicate another trend and another new role that seniors can learn. Older people might not yet have penetrated very far into the higher echelons of academic research, but there is no reason why this should not happen as senior academics seek to continue their research projects after they retire and also seek assistance from volunteers.

Older people can also become research students. Traditionally, young students commencing their academic careers undertake university research for higher degrees. One way into academia is by being a doctoral student, then a research assistant and finally achieving a junior lectureship. A more precarious university career has been that of a contract researcher, who has moved from one research project to another raising the research funding in each instance. However, with the development of lifelong learning, a new academic research path has been opening in US and UK universities. In the United Kingdom, the normal university career has been a three-year full-time baccalaureate degree, with some students continuing to a fourth year to complete their taught Masters degree. At the same time there have been two research degrees awarded by UK universities – the research Masters degree and the research Doctorate. These have traditionally been undertaken full-time by those students who have completed either their baccalaureate or their taught Masters degree and who have achieved very high grades. More recently, however, the taught Masters degree has been introduced in a part–time mode (and even a distance one), so that the one-year addition to the baccalaureate has become a two–year part–time taught degree, usually having a small research project as part of its curriculum. This part-time degree is being increasingly studied by professionals of all ages as part of their continuing professional education.

The other significant innovation has been that the research degrees have become part-time degrees which people in the professions have been able to undertake. In some instances, these part-time degrees have been undertaken in collaboration with the researcher's employers, so that an employee might have a senior manager – who is also academically very highly qualified – as a collaborative research supervisor with the university academic as the other supervisor.

Significantly, not all of these part-time research students are at the start of their careers; many have reached at least mid-career and some are even further advanced in their careers than this. Indeed, some of these part-time research students are reaching the end of their careers and, in fact, some retire from work long before they actually complete their research. In my own experience, I have been privileged to supervise research students from the fields of adult education, nurse and midwifery education, physiotherapy and human resource development, to the completion of their research degrees when they have reached the end of their career, or even after they have completed it. Many of these students have been extremely senior members of their profession; some having been awarded high national and international honours for services to their profession, including appearing on the Honours Lists. They are seniors, over the age of 55 years, and some closer to 70 years old, when they start their research. Many of them have then gone on to publish research papers as a result as part of their retirement occupation.

It is evident that those who have undertaken this research are at the apex of their careers rather than at the starting point. They are able to draw together their experience, undertake some research projects that younger researchers would not be able to complete and even get access to data that younger researchers would find difficult, even impossible, to obtain. More than one of them has told me that they see it as a way of contributing something more to the development of their own profession and, at the same time, providing them with a goal that takes them into retirement whilst still retaining a purpose to work within, and for, their profession. Clearly, the functions of undertaking research at the end of, or after the completion of, their careers needs more investigation but my impressions are that it provides a goal for those who have reached the highest echelons of their profession and demonstrates to them that they actually have the ability to achieve at the highest academic levels and give something back to their profession. For them, as for many others, work is not merely a means to an end, as some economists and politicians maintain. It has far deeper significance; it is a vocation in the wider religious sense of the term, and this needs much more research.

As the nature of the doctoral student undergoes change, the nature of the research supervision must be affected. In the first place, the supervisor is now the expert in research methodology, but not necessarily the expert in the subject being researched! The research student is the expert in the subject, and so research − like teaching − needs to become more student-orientated and the supervisor be recognized as not being the fount of wisdom about the subject being researched. Secondly, the expertise of seniors in their professions can compensate for not necessarily having achieved good honours in the baccalaureate examinations, since they have continued to learn throughout their professional lives. Universities have to become more flexible in their entry qualifications for part-time research degrees. Thirdly, the doctoral degree should not now only be regarded as a stepping stone to academic work. In a knowledge-based society there is an increasing number of professionals who are using knowledge all the time and some want to utilize their learning in undertaking research at a high level later in their careers and even as they draw them to an end. Finally, to state the almost unmentionable, undertaking a PhD after retirement can actually be a very stimulating hobby.

Conclusion

There is, then, a variety of ways in which seniors can continue to work and continue to learn both during the final years of their careers and into their retirement. As yet, there are not the types of opportunities for paid employment that there should be and a national resource is being wasted and will continue to be wasted while ageism is so prevalent in the work place. It is difficult to outlaw ageism, but it is less difficult to ensure that equal opportunity policies exist at work, which at least will make the playing field more equal.

Even so, work is not always so inspiring and vocational, and many people do wish to get away from it. The fact that they do is sometimes the fault of bad management, poor work design and so forth but there are, and probably always will be, some jobs that are less than stimulating. People occupying these jobs may sometimes find them mindless, as research about working on the factory floor on production lines has shown. Work can be alienating and destructive of our humanity, but all of us still continue to learn through our everyday lives and we continue to accumulate experience that we bring to the next experience in our lives – for this is what learning is. But it is also about the process of acquiring wisdom.

8

Learning meaning and wisdom

In the next two chapters we are going to deal with three interrelated ideas – meaning, wisdom and spirituality. All three of these terms have religious connotations, as we shall show below, and they clearly overlap with each other so that any division can only be for heuristic purposes. Meaning here refers to answers to ontological questions of the human condition and so it is a metaphysical, philosophical or theological term. Wisdom relates to understanding everyday life, although it is often seen as a religious term, since the concept occurs frequently in the Bible (Young, 1999). Spirituality, which will be discussed in the next chapter, refers to a specifically non-material domain of human being that in some ways transcends the cognitive.

Definition of meaning

The problem of meaning has been central to the human quest. It has hovered around the edges of learning theory without having been fully incorporated into it. Not all scholars have neglected this topic. For example, Mezirow (1988, p 233) tautologously defines meaning as 'a process of construing or appropriating a new or revised interpretation of the meaning of one's experience as a guide to decision and action' (also see Mezirow, 1991, pp 12–13). Likewise, according to Dahlgren (1984, pp 23–24) to 'learn is to strive for meaning, to have learned something is to have grasped its meaning.' Dahlgren seems to imply that experience has a meaning, while Mezirow suggests that we give meaning to experience – a constructivist position that is also taken in this book.

We have examined the idea of learning as a process of constructing experience in situations in which we find ourselves and reaching outcomes earlier, and we will not repeat this discussion here. However, the problem of meaning has not been fully incorporated into those earlier chapters and so we must first explore briefly the concept, and then we shall link it to understanding and truth. A much more extended discussion of this can be found in Jarvis (1992). What, then, is the meaning of meaning? The term has many definitions, including a metaphysical meaning and a socio-cultural one. It may be used as a noun and when it is used as a verb it conveys individual understanding or intention.

Metaphysical meaning: The quest to understand human existence has been with us since the beginning of recorded history. It is part of the human condition which we all experience. Fromm (1949, pp 44–45; original italics) summarizes this nicely:

> Man can react to historical contradictions by annulling them through his own action; but he cannot annul existential dichotomies, although he can react to them in different ways. He can appease his mind by soothing and harmonizing ideologies. He can try to escape from his inner restlessness by ceaseless activity in pleasure or in business. He can try to abrogate his freedom and to turn himself into an instrument of powers outside himself, submerging his self in them. But he remains dissatisfied, anxious, and restless. There is only one solution to his problem: to face the truth, to acknowledge his fundamental aloneness and solitude in a universe indifferent to his fate, to recognize that there is no power transcending him which can solve his problem for him. Man must accept responsibility for himself and the fact that only by using his own powers can he give meaning to life. But meaning does not imply certainty. Uncertainty is the very condition to impel man to unfold his powers. If he faces the truth without panic he will recognize that *there is no meaning to life except the meaning that man gives his life by the unfolding of his powers, by living productively*; and that only constant vigilance, activity, and effort can keep us from failing in the one task that matters – the full development of our powers within the limitations set by the laws of our existence. Man will never cease to be perplexed, to wonder, and to raise new questions. Only if he recognizes the human situation, the dichotomies inherent in his existence, and his capacity to unfold his powers will he be able to succeed in his task: to be himself and for himself and to achieve happiness by the full realization of those faculties which are peculiarly his of reason, love, and productive work.

Not everyone would accept this position since some sets of beliefs suggest that there is meaning to human existence (Hanfling, 1987a, 1987b), and that these are found through revelation. The endless quest for meaning to make sense of existence, however, is something that everyone understands, and which might well become more important to some of us as we age.

Socio-cultural meaning: Sometimes belief systems about human existence get embedded into our culture and we acquire them as young children. Luckmann, for instance, writes of a universe of meaning into which individuals are born and they acquire beliefs through the socialization process. He emphasizes (1967, p 44) the connections between the metaphysical and the non-transcendental and regards them as a total system: 'Symbolic universes are objectivated–meaning systems that relate the experiences of everyday life to a "transcendental" layer of reality. Other systems of meaning do not point beyond the world of everyday life; that is, they do not contain a "transcendental" reference.' These meaning systems reflect the sub-cultures into which we were born, and which we learn unreflectively and memorize. It is these early experiences that give rise to the birth of the conscious self, which helps us find our place in a specific social structure and social situation.

Meaning as a noun: Though we have been talking about systems of meaning, it is possible to use the term meaning much more specifically: words have meanings, situations have meanings, experiences have meanings, and so on. But words do not have meanings in themselves, nor do situations. Language is a system of arbitrary symbols. Nothing has intrinsic meaning; things only appear meaningful later in life because individuals grow up to take their universes of meaning for granted.

Meaning systems are socially constructed, but they are also situation-specific. Individuals have their own socially constructed and yet individualistic universes of meaning, and these are contained within their individual biographies. Hence different people may have different interpretations of a situation, and interpretations reflect something of both the interpreters and their social situation. Indeed, it follows from Bernstein's (1971) work that language might be used differently by different social groups. A simple example is that in American English the word elevator means the same as the word *lift* in British English. In British English an elevator is a mechanical hoist. Understanding how others use language and the meaning that they are trying to convey is part of the hermeneutic exercise. Achieving understanding is an outcome of the learning process. This understanding enables people to place their own meaning on a word, a situation, and so on. Meaning is, therefore, an outcome of learning and has to be linked conceptually to knowledge. People's individuality is reflected in the different meaning they attach to objects, events, and so forth, for understanding is being.

To mean: When people say that they mean something, they are trying to convey an understanding or express an opinion to other people. It is here in the verb to mean that the subjectivity of meaning is to be found. Communicating means seeking to share understandings, opinions, and attitudes with other people. Even when the word is used in the sense 'They meant to add it but they forgot,' the speaker's intention is still to make others understand the experience.

Meaning, then, is a complex concept, and it is difficult to provide a single definition. It contains elements of interpretation and of understanding – both aspects of
the learning process. Initially, however, meaning refers to interpretations of
human experience, and this is how we shall treat it here.

Luckmann (1967, p 50) suggests that the child becomes a 'self' by constructing
with others an 'objective and moral universe of meaning.' As such a universe of
meaning is constructed, many questions of meaning are posed. This process of
focusing on the 'unknowns' of human experience begins in early childhood
(Piaget, 1929) and appears to be fundamental to humanity. As the child's universe
expands, its questions of meaning change. For most people, trying to understand
the meaning of our existence is an intermittent but lifelong quest for most of us,
as we saw in the third chapter when we looked at Fowler's stages of faith.
Mezirow (1988, p 104) also argues that people move through a maturity gradient
during adulthood that involves a sequential restructuring of frames of reference
that enable them to construct meanings, and change occurs as the meaning
perspectives of others are adopted. Mezirow may not be correct when he suggests
that there is a maturity sequence, as though people are moving in a linear manner
through time, since, ultimately, it almost presupposes some form of predestina-
tion. Neither is he correct when he implies that people acquire new perspectives
through adopting those held by others, although this clearly happens very often
but ultimately it is an implicit denial of creativity.

This brief analysis demonstrates that, even though we are born into a universe
of meaning, we are still faced with questions, for which there are no ready
answers. We learn answers, but these are less definitive than they might have been
in an earlier period of history. Consequently, the quest that began in childhood
continues throughout life and, living in a multi-cultural society, we are increasingly aware that there are many systems of religious meaning and that no one
might offer the absolute truth. However, as institutionalized religious answers to
these questions of meaning have declined in significance, the human quest itself
has not disappeared but, if anything, gained a new importance in the contemporary world.

The mechanism of this quest is significant for our understanding of learning
throughout life. When people are in harmony with the world, when our meaning
system is sufficient to cope with the daily process of living, we are not faced with
the 'unknown' and so we can presume upon the world and need not learn. But if
we are suddenly confronted with a situation with which our meaning system
cannot cope – a disjunctural situation – we are forced to ask questions and learn.
It does not matter whether the unknown demands a major theological exposition
or merely a brief explanation from everyday experience. This desire to discover
meaning is fundamental to humanity, but is there a discoverable truth at the end
of this quest?

Truluck and Courtenay (1999, p 184) suggest that as adults age their quest
might not actually be for an ultimate truth but to identify and examine their basic

assumptions about life. It is a quest for a new world view as they need to refocus their lives as a result of major changes in it, such as retiring, losing one's independence, and so on. This might be achieved though contemplative learning or through discussion with others, deliberately or incidentally.

However, the question still remains for some: does objective truth exist, and are there phenomena that have unchanging and self-evident meaning? If objective truth exists, can people break through the cultural relativity to discover what is true beyond the confines of culture? If not, is everything relative? This seems to be one of the paradoxes of human existence. Children's 'why?' for every experience that they do not understand (Piaget, 1929) reveals the origin of this quest, and adults' 'why?' indicates that it continues throughout life. But are the answers that are discovered true? Can they be regarded as indisputable? Can they be verified? People want to treat their interpretations as if they are true; they want to regard the meanings that they impose on words and actions as if they are unchangeable. People appear to be conservative and seek security in meaningful answers and unchanging truths. Lifelong learning is a symbol of the way meaning unfolds with new experiences throughout life; it shows that people can keep seeking and finding meaning, but always there is new or deeper meaning that lies beyond it.

Meaning systems are relative, but they are often presented as if they were objective and unchanging; sometimes it is as if people collude in a delusion to feel secure. As Luckmann (1967) points out, everybody is born into a universe of meaning, and so it appears objective because this is their experience of it and it reflects the traditions of the culture into which they were born. But in order to fit into society, it is almost a prerequisite that people accept some of its pre-existing universe of meaning, even though this universe is socially constructed and might not always function in their own best interest. Sceptics are sometimes treated as outcasts because they throw doubt on what is generally accepted. But there is more than a good chance that in many situations the cultural answer will satisfy the questioners, and they may believe that they have acquired a meaningful answer. The apparent objectivity of the answer becomes a criterion for accepting it as true, or its functionality in the everyday world reinforces the idea that it is valid.

People hold beliefs, ideologies, an understanding of the world, a familiarity with culture and language that enable them to function meaningfully in their world. These beliefs and understandings become part of their biographies. Sometimes people recognize them as being relative and subjective, but others may regard them as objective and true. Within their experience, individuals have degrees of certainty about elements of their understanding: in some instances they are highly certain, but in others less so. They sometimes know something to be true, in other cases they believe it to be so, and at other times they think that it might be. In some situations, they are open to having their understanding changed, but in others, they may be less prepared to have their perspectives transformed. Such is the complexity of the human biography; its very structure reflects both the social background and the past experiences of every individual.

People are their biography, and as they enter potential learning situations throughout their lives, they seek to interpret them and respond to them, so that it might be claimed that all meaningful knowledge results from interpretation of experience, or that learning is the process of transforming experience into knowing or understanding. Through this process, individuals acquire understanding that they may regard as objective knowledge that is 'true'. This is what guides their actions, although they might realize that their beliefs are only relative and that they can learn and change their minds if they discover anything more satisfying. Some people are convinced that they have actually discovered truth, and nothing will change their minds but others rely on the fact that they are in agreement with other people and this sense of agreement reinforces their own position and legitimates it. If these support systems are removed, people may begin to doubt and this might be dispiriting in old age.

Indeed, there is a sense in which the structures of the world of work function as support systems. The very 'busyness' of life itself means that individuals continue to function, often without considering the questions of meaning since they have more immediate problems. However, after retirement, the meaning-giving function of work disappears; people might have more time on their hands and they are forced to ask these existential questions of meaning. This can be an exciting adventure as people seek to make sense of their lives, whereas for others it can be a time of uncertainty – as we saw earlier.

The process of discovering meaning usually teaches those who learn that more meaning exists beyond it. The very fact that still more meanings can be discovered indicates that the quest for meaning might not be meaningless. Meanings, however, are only relative and may in some way point to yet more sophisticated questions being asked and more sophisticated answers being given in this human quest that Fromm (1949) suggests has no ultimate answer. Bohm (1985, p 75) writes that:

> ... in physics, reflection on the meanings of a wide range of experimental facts and theoretical problems and paradoxes eventually led Einstein to new insights concerning the meaning of space, time, and matter, which are at the foundation of the theory of relativity. Meanings are thus seen to be capable of being organized into ever more subtle and comprehensive overall structures that imply, contain, and enfold each other in ways that are capable of indefinite extension – that is, one meaning enfolds another, and so on.

Consequently, the quest for ultimate meaning, truth, is like being on a journey that has no end and knowing this might well be one stage in the growth of wisdom. For others, wisdom might be the acceptance that there is no meaning to it.

The concept of wisdom

Wisdom is understandably a problematic concept at the present time – especially in its religious form – and the wisdom of the elders is almost generally regarded as defunct. The concept has also rarely been used in educational or learning literature. It is something that was relevant in traditional society when things did not change so fast and were not so technological as they are now. Consequently, the term has fallen into disfavour, but there have been a few attempts to return to it (Cochrane, 1995; Young, 1999). Cochrane (1995, pp 8–9) suggests that there are three different meanings of the term: individualistic, civic and cosmological. His cosmological definition has been briefly touched upon in the previous section of this chapter. His civic definition is utopian and reflected in the utopian idea of the learning society discussed briefly earlier in this book in which ideas of the good society, justice, fairness and the citizens' rights to participate in a democratic society, are central. However, our concern is more individualistic, since wisdom is no longer a generalizable concept; we are going to analyse it afresh and relate it to learning in everyday life. We are going to argue that wisdom is something learnt from experience rather than something that can be taught to others as a truth and utilized in their lives.

Wisdom is not an educational concept, nor is it something taught, but it occurs as the result of learning. *Collins Dictionary of the English Language* defines it as 'the ability or result of an ability to think and act utilizing knowledge, experience, understanding, common sense, and insight' and as 'accumulated knowledge, erudition, or enlightenment'. Wisdom is in some way the biographical store of knowledge, opinions, and insights gained, often through long years of life. Wisdom often implies being able to provide reasons for why things are the way they are, and in this sense it is metaphysical and cultural.

In this section we are going to explore the relationship between everyday experience and learning and then knowledge, everyday practical knowledge and wisdom and, finally, the value of the wisdom of elders in contemporary technological society.

Everyday experience and learning: Throughout our lives, many of these experiences are encountered, incorporated into our biographies. Or, as Schutz (1967, p 51) claims, 'I live *in* my Acts' and by reflecting upon them – which is outside the process of pure duration and a part of discontinuous time – we acquire meaning.

Everyday knowledge: We do not only learn knowledge but, as our definition has suggested, we also learn skills, attitudes, values, beliefs, emotions and the senses from our experiences. A great deal of the literature on learning has concentrated on knowledge but not all of it has analysed the different forms of knowledge. Scheler (1980, p 76), however, has suggested that there are seven types of knowledge:

- myth and legend – undifferentiated religious, metaphysical, natural and historical;
- knowledge implicit in everyday language – as opposed to learnt, poetic or technical;
- religious – from pious to dogmatic;
- mystical;
- philosophic-metaphysical;
- positive knowledge – mathematics, the natural sciences and the humanities;
- technological.

Scheler called his final two forms artificial because they change before they can become embedded in society's culture, although they are amongst the driving forces for global change. They are amongst the forces that help create the social conditions to which we are forced to adapt all the time, discussed earlier in the section on the learning society. Scheler's artificial forms reflect the knowledge of the knowledge society – a rapidly changing phenomenon, becoming so complex and differentiated, that it is hardly surprising that older people do not always manage to keep abreast with it all the time – but then neither do younger people!

The other five types of knowledge are part of everyday knowledge and are slower to change. Scheler formulated this list in the 1920s and clearly it is limited because in this knowledge society, knowledge itself has changed quite drastically. He did not discuss that type of everyday knowledge that we learn in order to cope with the exigencies of everyday – practical knowledge. As we age, so we learn a great deal of everyday knowledge from everyday experiences of our society and culture, and slowly older people gain a great deal of practical knowledge of the everyday.

However, this technological knowledge society is also generating another new form of everyday knowledge. For instance, the ability to use a personal computer and to keep on learning the program updates is still distinct from being able to understand how a computer works. There is a new everyday technical knowledge emerging which is distinct from the everyday practical knowledge. We are now in a position to elaborate on the seven forms of everyday knowledge, which exclude those two artificial forms that underlie and drive much of our advanced capitalist and global society:

- myth and legend – undifferentiated religious, metaphysical, natural and historical;
- religious – from pious to dogmatic;
- mystical;
- knowledge implicit in everyday language – as opposed to learnt, poetic or technical
- practical/functional knowledge of daily living;
- philosophic-metaphysical knowledge, including values;
- everyday technological knowledge.

Nevertheless, it is easy to see how older people can become alienated from some aspects of everyday life in this knowledge-based society if they do not feel at home with these new types of practical and technical knowledge and the skills required to utilize everyday appliances. Older people can, therefore, appear to be out-dated and unable to cope with contemporary society, so that the idea that older people are wise seems harder for some younger people to grasp. Since some older people, as do some middle-aged people, find it difficult to cope with this technical knowledge, and even more with the artificial positive and technological knowledge, they are consigned to the scrap heap and their accumulated learning treated as obsolete – like so many other things in this 'throwaway' world, where obsolescence is now designed into the system.

However, there is an active intent of many older people to keep up with this everyday functional knowledge in this society in which the rapidly changing positive and technological knowledge is emphasized. Although most formal adult learning is vocationally orientated, a greater percentage of older adults than any other age group who undertake adult education classes, do not have such an orientation in their learning (Beinhart and Smith, 1997, 176). Learning to use the computer and the World Wide Web are among the most popular subjects studied by the elderly. Their other interests tend to be in cultural subjects and the humanities – non-vocationally orientated – since learning is for learning's sake. Yet it is through the study and research, such as local history research groups, that third age learning can help to preserve and articulate the cultural values of society.

Despite not always being able to cope with positive and technical knowledge (artificial knowledge), many do have the knowledge learnt from their experiences of everyday life, knowledge that they know works for them. As we pointed out above, everyday knowledge is pragmatic knowledge – it is practical and functional. Heller (1984) actually suggests that everyday knowledge is always opinion and never scientific knowledge, but that depends on how scientific is defined and here the definition seems to be too narrow. Science is a matter of exploration and experiment – this we all do throughout our lives and it is through the process of trial and error in everyday living that we have acquired the practical knowledge and skills that we have. In this sense living is itself an experiment and as we age so we reach certain conclusions about living. Many of these we constantly test in the process of daily life and they are found to work, or else we are in situations of disjuncture and discontinuity when we realize that we are forced to learn new things – which most of us are doing much of the time.

People develop and mature from all of these experiences – for learning is fundamental to the process of human development. However, not all pragmatic learning produces the 'correct' solution. Consider the following illustration. Through a self-directed learning exercise, a person acquires the skills to repair a problem in an old car. However, the fault recurs, and the second time it is easier to repair the fault, because the lessons learnt on the previous occasion are put to use. Experience is a useful reservoir for future learning. The next time the fault occurs, it seems even easier to repair than the previous time, because of the experiences gained on the previous two occasions. A pattern for the repair emerges, a form of habitualization, and each time the fault occurs it gets easier to repair it. The only trouble is that the fault keeps recurring because the self-directed learning exercise did not completely solve the problem in the first place, and the pattern that evolved to repair the fault became habitualized. Yet, there is always the possibility of learning to repair the fault another way and becoming more proficient in car repair, and so on.

The knowledge we have of everyday life is pragmatic – we know that it works for us. Even that metaphysical knowledge that relates to ethics and values is pragmatic – we know that this value system works for us – we can live with it and with ourselves for having adopted it. Much of our everyday knowledge is actually embedded in culture, but we go on creating new knowledge for ourselves as we live through the experiences of everyday life, and what makes our society a learning society is that a greater proportion of the knowledge that we use everyday has to be learnt from these experiences rather than from the culture into which we are born. Yet those forms of knowledge that Scheler referred to as positive and technological knowledge still lie beyond the everyday and, in this sense, they are still artificial and are changing even more rapidly.

We shall return to some of these aspects of everyday knowledge in the next chapter, but for the present we can see that there are a number of dimensions, or forms of knowledge, included in everyday knowledge. The older we are and the more experiences we have had, the greater the foundation of everyday knowledge that we have to guide the way we act. It is this that constitutes the basis of wisdom.

Wisdom: This is a synthesis of all of these seven forms of knowledge learnt from experiences of everyday life and incorporated into our own maturing biography. But the wisdom gained is each person's own theory about living and reality. It is subjective, whereas wisdom has traditionally been regarded as objective and possessed by all older people. 'In the later years, the imposed expectations for changes in work/retirement and the innate drive to refocus induces reintegration of cognitive and social repertoires. Havighurst... described this as a refocusing of one's past into the present in order to derive *meaning of life* for the present: the act of reviewing one's 'biography' and, potentially, the emergence of wisdom.' (Thornton, 1986, p 74.)

Moody (1986, p 127) also highlights this process: 'Those older people commonly judged 'wise' are those who respond to genuinely novel situations by applying the lessons of experience in an entirely new context. They do not abandon past experience, but they apply their learning analogically.' He notes that there is a return to story-telling to assist people in their search for meaning in this rapidly changing, technological world. As we have already discussed, he also recognizes that there are some older people whose learning and actions have become habitualized, so that their reactions to new experiences are rigid. They are unable to respond to change, and so they take refuge in not learning.

However, older people are able to use their past learning, their biography, to understand and cope with many contemporary situations. Whilst this does not apply to every situation or to every form of knowledge, it does apply to those forms of knowledge that are embedded in society's culture and learnt from everyday life. They have acquired a practical understanding of the world – practical knowledge, skills, attitudes, beliefs, values, emotions and senses – and we examined this process of maturation in the third chapter. Older, mature people have learnt pragmatically what works for them, and also some of the things that do not. It is their learning and it might, or might not be useful, to others. And it is their own wisdom – something that is subjective – but it may not be recognized by others, especially those of younger generations; neither might it be useful to them. Heller (1984, pp 165–215) examines the relationship between knowledge and everyday life. She (1984, p 166) acknowledges this when she writes that: 'the best example of… adopting a theoretical attitude toward the world in relation to the world of things is provided by cases of failure, lack of success; when a method I have used over and over again fails to work, the pragmatic attitude itself, the desire for efficiency, makes me stop and ask 'Why?' 'What has gone wrong?' and at once I am thinking along theoretical lines.'

The significance of this claim is at least threefold. First, we see that, as we have argued throughout this book, learning begins when there is a disjuncture between biography and experience that leads to a questioning attitude. Second, everyday knowledge is pragmatic in nature. Learning from primary experience results in pragmatic knowledge, and this is also true whether the situation involves professional practice or everyday experience. The learning gained makes us even more experienced. This is the way that everyday knowledge is learnt and everyday beliefs are acquired. Third, we develop a theoretical orientation toward the world which we shall suggest is precisely the nature of wisdom – it is, as it were, a theory of life. Elsewhere it has been argued (Jarvis, 1999a) that in the workplace, individuals have to generate their own theory from practice and that they have to take what they learn from other sources and try it out for themselves. What was traditionally called theory has become information that practitioners can use and try out in their professional practice to see if it works for them. When it works, they incorporate their learning into their own theory of practice. This is also true of all people's learning about everyday life – it is everyday wisdom and as we mature so it develops.

Elders do have a great deal more experience of the everyday that is useful to them but it cannot be assumed to be valid or useful to others. It will also be recalled from the fourth chapter that Cattell (1963), and Cattell and Horn in subsequent work, developed a theory of fluid and crystallized intelligence, in which they argued that crystallized intelligence increased with experience. Older people do have more crystallized intelligence, they have had more emotional experiences, and they have learnt to live with ambiguity and contradiction, and so on.

Consequently, it is suggested here that those elders who have learnt from their life's experiences have developed a theory of life that works for them. It is subjective and individual and whatever the advice or guidance that elders give to others, it can be no more than information that has to be tried out in the recipient's life. Many elders will have developed their own wisdom but its possession is not their automatic right and neither is it an objective phenomenon.

The value of the wisdom of the elders: To know that we have accumulated knowledge and skill gives individuals a sense of personal worth which is important in itself. In this sense, understanding one's own wisdom is of value in itself – it provides a sense of integrity to our personhood. To have reached the stage in life where we value life itself and the world in which we live for no other reason than that we are alive and live in the world, where we can treasure being itself and appreciate the wonder of existence, is of great value. Perhaps, above all, this is where wisdom lies. No longer do we have to conquer the world, only to recognize that we have a part to play within it. But once we have achieved this state we are, paradoxically, in a position to demonstrate our wisdom to others – to show precisely why the wisdom of the elders is still valuable.

Older people have memories of the culture of a society and can, perhaps, see better the implications for some of the things happening in society than some younger people still caught up in the process of pursuing their careers and being responsible for their families. For younger people, living is still about finding their way through the journey of life. The adventure is by no means over as we age, but perhaps we have learnt to treat it a little differently and even to tread the path a little more judiciously, even though we are only too well aware that we are closer to the journey's end. But it is because we are where we are that we can play our part in society. We can help it preserve the heritage that has been vested in us through our learning and living our lives.

We can pass on to others the fruits of our learning, but now we have to recognize its status. It is personal, subjective knowledge that may, or may not, be applicable to other people. Older people are, as we showed earlier, potential mentors (Daloz, 1986) for any who wish to seek advice and support. But, mentoring is not teaching but a process of using one's wisdom to support another. However, it is unfortunate that, unlike the experts in the world of work, they are often not called on to share their expertise – even in that industrial world in which many of them worked for so long. The society in which the elders have functioned has changed beyond recognition so that their biographical experience may be discounted by some. When this occurs, individuals who have gained a great understanding of the practical wisdom that is still embedded in society's culture are denied the opportunity to demonstrate their usefulness.

Older people can also volunteer to undertake jobs in those sectors of society which governments and other bodies do not fund adequately, thereby demonstrating the inappropriateness of such priorities. However, there is an important caveat to be made here – older people should not be seen as a substitute for governmental and civic involvement in such activities, but as a symbol of the priorities of human society and of social living. In addition, they can undertake research and put on the national agenda, those local and national problems that older people regard as important but that neither government nor industry will fund and prefer to sweep under the table. In a sense, the freedom of older people gives them the power to influence the public agenda in a variety of ways.

There are a number of areas in which older adults can demonstrate and use their wisdom but four have been emphasized throughout this book. We can, for instance:

- help preserve society's culture through what we continue to value;
- pass on to others what we have learnt and value through acting as mentors;
- help to create a better society and the good life through our own social activities – through both volunteering and social activism;
- emphasize those dimensions of human life, such as the spiritual and aesthetic, that tend to get under-emphasized by the demands and values of contemporary society.

Conclusion

We have argued in this chapter that wisdom is personal and subjective, learnt throughout life but not necessarily applicable to other's lives, so that it cannot just be taught to them as if it were truth. Clearly wisdom incorporates the quest for meaning; it often implies being able to provide reasons for why things are the way they are, and in this sense it is metaphysical and pre-sociological. It explains the 'thus-ness' (Heller, 1984, p 214) of this world. Heller (1984, p 212) suggests that it stems from a form of contemplative learning that could occur only after humankind had conquered the physical hardships of survival: 'The emergence of contemplation as an independent mental attitude depends on man's having attained a state of existence beyond the struggle for mere survival... The world in which he lives and moves awakens man's interest and curiosity. And whenever there is neither need for, nor possibility of a pragmatic attitude, man's [interest and] curiosity become ends in themselves. Anything that is of pragmatic interest in one coordinate system can become an object of contemplation in another.'

Perhaps it was not only in the early world that humankind was able to contemplate the meaning of existence only when it had overcome the basic struggles to exist. Even today, it is only in the later stages of life, when people are freed from many of the constraints of contemporary society and when they own their own space, that they are able to stop and contemplate and to come to terms with life. Certainly there is something metaphysical in this idea, although it is as much a psychological process as it is a metaphysical one. It might be a manifestation of spirituality or religiosity, but it is not necessarily something that could be called Christian or Muslim or Buddhist. Having the ability to provide an explanation for the way that the world works and also to explain its 'thus-ness' lies at the heart of wisdom. Indeed, this is the basis of philosophy – the love of wisdom. The possession of wisdom was much treasured in the ancient world, because the sages had contemplated the nature of existence and then they taught others who learned from them. Wise people were nearly always old, since they had accumulated the experiences and learned knowledge which was then incorporated into their own lives. But this was, of course, probably less true of the Greek philosophers who developed the art of philosophical contemplation and made it a way of life.

Nevertheless, having contemplated the everyday for many years does result in the acquisition of a body of knowledge, a theory, that is more orientated to life itself than to the technical and positive knowledge that Scheler called artificial. It is this endeavour to understand life itself that also lies at the heart of religion. Despite the apparently secular society in which we live, it is crucial that we recognize that religion, defined in this broader sense, is still almost universal. It is only Christianity in the West that appears to be declining. This universal quest to understand life manifests itself in most people, especially as we age.

Wisdom itself, however, is no longer seen as something universally applicable just because it has been learnt throughout the life of the elderly. It has to be tested by others to whom it is offered and found to be useful before it can be claimed to be valid. Its status has changed and it is no longer truth, merely information that might be useful. The status of the elderly has, therefore, changed from something that is ascribed to something that is achieved. Older people gain the respect of others if they and their wisdom are seen to be valuable to society and this they have to demonstrate through the advice and support they are able to render, in their priorities in social living and through their integrity with themselves.

There is the danger in this changing situation, especially if some of the learning of the elderly is rejected, that the elderly themselves will be rejected; that their personhood will no longer be respected, merely because they are old. Society has to learn to differentiate between the person and the person's usefulness to society. There might be some grounds for rewarding people with higher status who contribute more than others to the good of society, but the humanity and personhood of everybody in society needs to be equally respected and enhanced, whatever their age.

9

Learning spirituality

As we said at the start of the last chapter, these two chapters cover overlapping topics. In a sense they both relate to religion in some way but because they overlap we have had to explore the manner in which we are using the terms in this book. In the first part of this chapter, therefore, we will highlight the differences that we see between religion and Christianity – although the same discussion would hold good for Islam and the other institutionalized religions. In the third chapter we looked at Fowler's work on faith development and we suggested that in its higher stages it pointed beyond Christianity; it is this that we will develop in the second part of this chapter. Here we will suggest that spirituality underlies religion itself and we will also explore the process of learning spirituality, especially in relation to ageing.

Religion and Christianity

When Christianity was the taken-for-granted truth – at the time when Western society was dominant – it became easy to confuse religion and Christianity and this has most certainly occurred in the United Kingdom. However, in this multi-cultural, multi-faith world the fallacy of this should become self-evident. Even so, we have to recognize that older people brought up in a society where one institution has been dominant, like Christianity in the United Kingdom, might not make the distinction between the two and, indeed, some believers still make the same exclusive claims for Christianity that have been made in the past. Now however, fewer people will be inclined to accept them. Christianity is but one cultural manifestation, albeit a very significant one, of humankind's wider religiosity. There is no intention here to enter into a theological debate about these claims, only to point out that there is a fundamental difference between the concepts of religion and Christianity, and while older people brought up in the Christian faith might find their meaning and solace in it, others might not. Consequently, it is important when we consider older people's learning to recognize that they may not all need to be taught about the Christian or Islamic answers to human existence, so much as to be encouraged and supported as they seek to discover meaning and spirituality for themselves. Elsewhere (Jarvis, 1999a), I have argued that the Christian Church needs to expand its mission to recognize the wider religiosity of people and provide opportunity for them to explore it.

However, the difference between religion and Christianity needs to be clearly delineated. Religion has had many definitions, almost as many as there have been scholars writing about it. Among the most well known are the following: 'Religion is a set of coherent answers to the core existential questions that confront every human group.' (Bell, 1980, p 333.) and 'Religion is the human enterprise by which a sacred cosmos is established.' (Berger, 1969, p 26.) (Both definitions cited in Turner, 1991.)

Implicit in these two definitions are two main standpoints. The first implies that there is a set of answers that might be taught and learnt but, in the second, that there is a human quest in order to establish the answers. Turner (1991, p 242), commenting on a minimum approach to religion as a belief in spiritual beings, says that religion arose from attempts of primitive people 'to make sense of their own mental experiences' – that is, to learn about their own lives. Religion then, according to Turner, stems from humankind's response to the unanswerable existential experiences. In contrast, other interpreters might want to claim that religion is the belief in the set of coherent answers that stem from this quest.

This is important inasmuch as there are times in history when individual teachers propose coherent sets of answers to these questions and, if they are accepted and gain a following, their answers gradually become codified, docu-mented and institutionalized. Churches, faiths and institutionalized religions sometimes emerge as a result of such teachers and teachings, although this does not occur every time a religious teacher appears on the scene, since many sets of teachings have been expounded which have never become institutionalized. However, where the faiths have grown and the Churches become powerful, notably Christianity and Islam in the West, then the codified theologies have assumed forms of orthodoxy that have then been taught as truth. These systems have never been totally unified, since the institutions themselves have been torn asunder by theological and other divisions. Even so, the organizations that have become established within institutionalized religion have not only proclaimed their faith through preaching, and established mechanisms through which it might be taught; the Churches have educational missions to teach their belief systems.

This division between the institutional teaching and the individual quest needs to be clearly recognized since there are times in most individuals' lives when they realize their own mortality and begin to ask quite fundamental questions about the meaning of their own lives. This is a form of maturation and there are at least three or four times in an older person's life when this questioning process is most likely to occur: at the so-called mid-life crisis, at retirement, at times of personal crisis and loss and during the final years of life. The questions – Why should this have happened to her? Why has this happened to me? Why did I not do that when I had a chance? and so on, are the disjunctural questions which might constitute the start of a learning process, as we argued in the second chapter when we examined human learning.

In a bygone age in the United Kingdom, it would have been assumed that people would have sought a Christian answer to their questions, but this assumption is no longer justified since we live both in a multi-faith and a non-Christian society. Many older people who have been brought up within an institutionalized religion, such as Christianity, might seek traditional answers because they have always accepted it as true. But for others who have rejected it, there is still a religious quest to be undertaken. For those still able to pursue their own quest, seeking to learn about the different institutional religions might become an enriching activity.

But in the case of other older people, who are being cared for, it is necessary to enquire whether the individuals have had a religious background. When they have had such an upbringing, a sympathetic response within an institutional framework might be a wise reaction. It might not be justifiable to cause the elderly to doubt what they have learnt in the past and to which they have current belief-orientations, since they may not want or cannot to go through a whole new learning process. But for some friends or carers this might constitute an ethical question since they do not accept the same beliefs. In this case a sympathetic response and a promise to get a chaplain or priest of the relevant faith to talk with the older person might be the most loving response. For those who have not got this belief-orientation, discussions with a priest, or a counsellor, or sympathetic friends might form part of the learning process.

It is significant that the distinction between religion and Christianity is recognized in one of the few studies on religion and later life that has been published, but it is not really developed there. For instance, Howse (1999, p 7) writes:

> It is evident, however, that a religious outlook, even perhaps a specifically Christian outlook, may flourish outside the body of active churchgoers, and in spite of the waning authority of the Churches. It is an important part of the Christian tradition that there is more to true religion than conformity to prescribed ritual observances and creeds. It should have far-reaching ramifications for the way people live their lives, for what they feel and think and do about all aspects of their situation in life. Impatience with rigid requirements for practice and belief might perhaps cause many people to detach themselves from any kind of organized Christianity... while remaining loyal to what they see as its *essential* teachings. [Italics in original.]

Howse has surveyed a great deal of sociology of religion literature and rightly concludes (1999, p 104) that it does point out the fact that religion plays a greater part in well-being in later life and that carers should recognize this, although, naturally, he restricts his discussion to the institutional Christian faith. Perhaps this is something that the Churches themselves need to recognize and, as well as appointing youth workers, they might consider appointing staff to work with the growing number of older people in our society – third age workers.

In the new global society we know a great deal more about other people's beliefs, and so we actually have more opportunities to learn different answers to our questions and different practices surrounding every stage of life. We can visit different places, experience different cultures and learn about the many answers given to the questions of meaning. However, it is important to recognize here that belief systems are cognitive and we were careful in the third chapter to point out that there are other dimensions to human being as well, as we also learn these. Institutional religions recognize this and, to varying extents, they have a broader spiritual dimension.

Spirituality

In the first section we have implied that many religious systems are belief systems – and this is certainly the element that has been most emphasized in the West, although it has been recognized in the Christian Churches that orthodox belief no longer really exists. There is a wide variety of interpretations. However, we have also discussed religion itself in terms of belief systems, whereas religion has another dimension – spirituality.

Spirituality is not about belief in supernatural beings, ghosts or anything like that. It is another dimension of humankind. It is about us, as human beings, plumbing the depths of our experience, of our being, seeking to both understand and love existence itself. In this we discover the sacredness of life itself and, ultimately, we endeavour to contemplate Being itself. Spirituality is about living itself. Hart and Horton (1993, p 241) write: 'The spiritual... suffuses a person's entire existence within the world, integrating not only her entire organism as a unified system, but integrating her into the world as a whole... Thus, as an ongoing process, spirituality requires and simultaneously moves the individual toward self and community integration.' For them, spirituality has at its basis a love that values the self, affirms the community and integrates the two in being itself. They were actually writing about a learning community, but it is clear throughout their writing the spirituality is learnt in the maturation process.

Metropolitan Anthony of Sourozh (1999) writes about the spirituality of old age, depicting elements of this learning process. He shows how older people have to come to terms with past events in their lives and, as it were, learn to live with themselves. He (1999, p 31) suggests that: 'It is given to us to live and relive, to be forced back into situations of our past which were wrong, painful or distorted, so that from the new maturity that we possess we can undo them, resolve them as one can undo a knot and let things go.'

He makes the telling point that people do need to learn from their contemplation. This, it will be recalled, is one of the reflective learning processes that we discussed in our model of learning in the second chapter. If we look back to that model, we can see that individuals can start with their memories and recreate a new experience upon which they can reflect again since they have more mature biographies. We shall return to this theme in the next chapter when we discuss reminiscence.

Metropolitan Anthony goes on to show that individuals can develop their own spirituality in relationship – for it is only in relationship that love can exist and develop. (I have developed this within a discussion of ethics and education for adults elsewhere – Jarvis, 1997.) It is in discovering human being – being itself – that people develop their own spirituality. However, not all people enjoy such close interpersonal relationships; contemporary society has fragmented, and Giddens (1991, pp 31–32) comments on this phenomenon: 'Modernity, it might be said, breaks down the protective framework of the small community and of tradition, replacing these with much larger, impersonal organizations. The individual feels bereft and alone in a world in which she or he lacks the psychological supports and the sense of security provided by more traditional settings. Therapy offers someone to turn to, a secular version of the confessional.'

In a sense it might be suggested that spirituality is something totally different from the discussion of the previous two chapters because this does not require belief in a specific institutionalized religion. In this modern secular world, this essential dimension of humanity will no doubt take on a number of new manifestations in the near future. Likewise, it is hardly surprising that the counselling professions have assumed a much more significant place in some people's lives and have assumed the role of a secular priesthood.

Psychiatrists, likewise, understand the importance of this dimension of our existence, for in caring for people who have not been able to develop into mature and whole people, they have discovered that the spiritual dimension of humankind is necessary for the maturation process. How do people mature? In earlier chapters of this book, we have looked at the way people mature through different forms of learning and at the significance of interpersonal relationships. It is clear from this discussion of spirituality that these interpersonal relationships are a significant part of the maturation process, in which we learn to take into ourselves those whom we love and through which we mature emotionally. But the spiritual dimension is different from all of these – it is about religious wonder. Vaillant (1993, p 337) writes thus:

Mature defences grow out of our brain's evolving capacity to master, assimilate, and to feel grateful for life, living, and experience. Such gratitude encompasses the capacity to wonder. To see and comprehend the joy of a sunset or a symphony or to sustain a mature religious conviction is evidence that one's mind has experienced a hallucination or an illusion of sorts. Such wonder is in itself a transformation and a self-deception of the most sublime nature. But how does such wonder develop? How shall we understand such paradoxical hope – the health promoting, morale-restoring self-deception that transforms the lonely atheist in a foxhole into a true believer?

In the United States, personal growth workshops have been introduced which involve the physical and the mental. Luce (1979), founder of Senior Actualization and Growth Exploration (SAGE) regards their underlying philosophy as responding to old age, a time to discover 'inner richness for self-development and spiritual growth' (cited in Waters and Goodman, 1990, p 190).

We may not agree with Vaillant that these experiences are hallucinations or self-deception but we might well accept that they are of a most sublime wonder. However, Vaillant suggests that there are four major ways in which we can develop our spirituality, which he says are through dreaming, sacred places, play and integration of thought and emotion. He points out that:

- Dreaming (day and night) is essential for us to master time, to develop defences and to wonder. But he does not use dreaming just like night-time dreams but about visions and removing ourselves a little from the hard world of reality, but in night-time dreams we can reflect on the past but do nothing about it, while in visions we can look to the future with hope. They can be creative. Great leaders catch this latter dimension of people's existence, such as Martin Luther King's dream of a better world for blacks in the United States. It is not insignificant that dreaming is the aboriginal word for the sacred writings.
- Sacred places allow us to imagine, to sustain paradox, and to wonder. In sacred places wonder reigns supreme – here we can wonder at the mystery of the divine, be attracted by the symbols and we can step outside of the ordinary. Here is the mystery of our humanity. The sacred place need not be a church or another building, and whilst I understand the movement away from holy buildings we do need to find our own sacred places – places of great beauty, personal significance or of community importance. The more profound our spirituality, the more the whole world becomes a sacred place.
- Play can also remove us from the world of reality; it also allows us to create order out of chaos. Play can help us put into the world things that were not there and allows us to create our own reality. Play is a much wider concept and as we age we do not play in the sense that children play but play can, and

does, become ritual and we need our rituals. In ritual or sacrament the players accept a transformed identity, almost in a mystic unity. For instance, in the Christian sacrament of holy communion the penitent becomes the forgiven.

●   We need to link the world of thought with that of emotion, which we also do in rituals, in play and in dreams. Reason and emotion are joined in dreaming, sacred places and ritual performances, and so on. The cognition is united with the emotions – sorrow and distress but also happiness and joy – they are individually experienced but shared together.

Vaillant (1993, p 344) suggests that: 'Religion, psychotherapy, and spiritual reawakening all facilitate the identifications and improved morale that permit the ego integration required for mature defences.'

As we age, then, the spiritual dimension of life enables us to transcend the problems of having no further horizons or mountains to climb and the frailties of the body. It enables us to appreciate existence itself. Sometimes we need to be alone in our quest and at other times we need to be with others. But it would be true to say that this is a dimension of our lives that is least discussed and, consequently, among the functions of the carer, the educator and the priest is that of facilitating such opportunities. If the Churches could break away from their theological formulations and reach into the depths of human spirituality, they might actually discover the prevalence of religion in this apparently secular age. They might also begin to provide a fundamental opportunity for all people, of whatever age or persuasion – although especially the more elderly, to discuss the undiscussable questions.

Indeed, it would be true to say that the poverty of the rational, cognitive and scientific approaches to human existence that have emerged from the Enlightenment demand that this dimension of our lives be more thoroughly explored and, as people age, so this dimension grows in importance. This is slowly being recognized and at the time when I was revising the drafts of this book, *Spiritual Intelligence* by Danah Zohar and Ian Marshall (2000) was published. In this they recognize three forms of intelligence – cognitive, emotional and spiritual – which together produce the rounded human being. They are also concerned to draw together the thinking from different cultures and religious traditions and locate spirituality at the heart of each human being. Clearly such publications indicate both the poverty of Western rationality and the need for Western culture to rediscover the spiritual. They also indicate the need that people have to develop this dimension of their being.

Conclusion

While older people are strong and active they are able to use their leisure time in many ways, to develop themselves and to help others. As they get older, they might begin to lose the use of their bodies and then they are forced back to their inner selves and to appreciate those whom they love and who love them – those who care for them. In being forced to contemplate the meaning of life they enter the spiritual dimension and as we lose the full use of our physical powers we have to learn to be more dependent on others but also to be more dependent on our inner resources. In the following chapters we will turn to the fourth age.

10

Learning mental fitness

One of the greatest fears that most of us have as we age is that of losing our mental prowess, and for many years it has been assumed that, for many people, there has not been a great deal that we can do to prevent this occurring. But the message of this chapter is that 'if you do not use it, you will lose it', since it is now recognized that there is a lot that we can do to slow down the decline in our mental abilities. There is a great deal of research to demonstrate this – too much to include in this one chapter! It has also been argued that crystallized intelligence can still increase as we age for many, so long as we stay involved in the world. We began to explore this in Chapter 6 when we categorized older adults into three groups: the sages, the doers and the harmony seekers. We did, however, deliberately omit those who were mentally unwell. However, the distinction between the learners and the doers is rather crude, since there is evidence that keeping a healthy body helps generate a healthy mind as well, and this we shall explore further in the first section of the chapter. Thereafter, we shall examine the relationship between social involvement and mental fitness, then, look at research undertaken on mental fitness and, finally, we shall elaborate on empowering adults to assume responsibility and to be involved in their wider social context. In the concluding discussion we shall point to the need for a new category of therapist – the learning therapist – and suggest that all carers should become learning therapists.

Physical and mental fitness

The crude distinction between the sage and the doer that I drew earlier almost presupposes that there is a separation between body and brain, but this is clearly not true. The brain is a part of the body – it has physical dimensions. Although this is not true for the mind, the state of the mind is dependent on the state of the neurological phenomenon that houses it. But because the body and brain are both physical, the condition of the body impinges on the functioning of the brain. James and Coyle (1998, p 39) suggest that:

... since the brain accounts for some 25 per cent of blood circulatory activity (despite representing a far smaller percentage of body weight and tissue) maintenance of cardiovascular fitness, through aerobic exercise, may entrain particular benefits for the brain and hence cognitive processes, including memory. Ivy *et al* (1992) review literature that points to reduced blood circulation and deterioration of the blood–brain barrier with age, both of which may be associated with tissue loss and impaired cognitive functioning.

In a similar manner, Gardner (1983, p 48) makes the point that malnutrition is also associated with 'deleterious consequence for both emotional and cognitive functioning'. Ivy *et al* made the point, however, that the direction of causality between biology and cognition is a major question. But Labouvie-Vief (1985, p 257) suggests that 'no significant portion of variance in intellectual behaviour may be accounted for by a readily demonstrated maturational change *as long as* subjects are in reasonably good health and/or living in the community.' [*Italics* in the original.]

She notes that it is hard to demonstrate causality with normal, healthy adults and so she espouses the theory of discontinuity, first enunciated by Birren (1963), in which physiological factors only become the major determining ones in cognitive behaviour when they reach critical abnormal stages, such as approaching death. She feels that there is a much more complex relationship between them, and she agrees that there might be a biological component in some forms of cognitive decline, such as psychomotor speed being related to the lack of physical exercise. She cites the research by Botwinick and Thompson (1971) in support of this position. James and Coyle (1998, p 44) also argue from their own research that 'cardiovascular fitness is a more influential factor in modulating aspects of memory performance than in affecting other aspects of cognitive activity'. Consequently, they point to the potential advantages of regular physical activity for mental well-being.

Hence, the growth in physical exercise clubs and classes that have a programme for the elderly is a welcome move. However, there are less formal types of physical exercise that are also beneficial. Some U3As, for instance, organize regular rambles and other forms of exercise. In some sheltered accommodation, opportunities to have a small space of the garden also encourage regular physical activity and even in residential homes there may be organized physical exercises. Nevertheless, there is also research that suggests that involvement in continuing education is beneficial to the physical well-being of the participants. Panayotoff (1993) analysed 114 elders engaged in four separate educational programmes and discovered that there was a beneficial effect on the physical well-being of the participants at the end of the course, but that within six weeks of the courses' completion the benefits had disappeared. This suggests perhaps that the mental involvement needs to be an ongoing process if it is to contribute to physical well-being.

Social involvement and mental fitness

Earlier in this book we looked at learning from everyday life but there are those people who are in danger of disengaging from the everyday as they age, and these we suggested are the harmony seekers. Research has shown, however, that there are positive advantages of staying involved and we shall look at just four forms of involvement here: games, engagement in everyday activities, engagement in the 'Keep on talking' programme in Australia and, finally, lifelong learning.

Games: Traditionally in children's education it has been recognized that joining in games enables them to learn to become team players, appreciate others and to develop a sense of fair play. Little research has been undertaken into the reasons why older adults play games, such as cards and dominoes. Does games playing still provide learning opportunities for the players? It was this question that Mangrum and Mangrum (1995) addressed when they analysed some games of dominoes in a senior citizens' centre in the United States. They (1995, p 244) discovered that: 'During the game talk, they (the elders) seemed to be saying, This is me, this is who I am, and this is how I would like to be thought of.'

In a sense the game provides the opportunity for elders to construct, or the present, positive self-images that are important for their own integrity. Mangrum and Mangrum (1995, pp 244–45) also conclude that: 'Quality of life depends on a lifetime of learning. This study shows that games play a significant role in learning for all generations. Game playing is more than recreation... a pleasurable use of discretionary time... or a commentary on the social order... it may be an opportunity for teaching the elderly the importance of life-enhancing behaviours, such as maintaining a positive self-concept and understanding the stages of coping with loss.' We should, consequently, be encouraging games playing in older peoples' centres and residential care homes in order to provide opportunity for incidental learning through such social activities. We shall return to the use of games and puzzles later in this chapter.

Everyday social activities: We have already alluded to Chène's (1994) study of the importance of being with others (Chapter 6), which was also important in the analysis of the games of dominoes discussed above. There is a great deal of research which shows that being with others acts as a stimulus for all those in the interaction, enabling them to recall past events and share their experiences with others. Furthermore, we are able to find our identity in relation to others. As we have shown throughout this book, it is in the everyday that there are both planned and incidental learning opportunities. Once we create a world upon which we can presume, we stop learning.

Keep on talking: This is a lifelong learning programme devised in Australia (Worrall *et al*, 1998) for small groups of older people who are concerned about communication skills. The programme covers:

● discussion about communication and well-being;
● coping with hearing loss, services and listening devices for the hard of hearing;
● maintaining literacy skills;
● memory;
● a summary session.

The idea underlying the programme was to provide information, to get the participants to communicate and to take further action to ensure that they maintained their communication activity. The outcome of the programme was that the participants learnt about communication but also that, in the year following its completion, a considerably higher proportion of the participants took active steps to ensure that they maintained their communication capacities.

There have been similar types of programmes provided by educators of older adults on other specific subjects, such as memory loss (Foos, 1997), devised to lower anxiety levels by providing specific information about memory, Alzheimer's disease and techniques for remembering. These programmes are necessary to help allay fears and also to help older people utilize techniques to improve their lifestyle.

Involvement in lifelong learning: Cusack (1996, p 315) shows how involvement in a lifelong learning project resulted in the participants feeling:

● less depressed;
● that although their bodies might be failing they could still learn;
● enjoyment;
● more able to interact and help others.

The fact that the seniors were involved in planning the educational programme also meant that their self-esteem was enhanced since they thought that the views that they expressed were being heard. Hickson and Housley (1997, p 542) also argue how creativity can be nurtured in lifelong learning programmes and they cite Dawson and Baller's (1972) conclusions that 'older adults who participated in creative activities may live longer, (have) healthier lives, (and suffer) less debility over time than their age cohorts not involved in the arts'.

Improving mental fitness

The advantages of physical fitness are well known, although the idea of mental fitness is something much more new but no less important. However, there has been a widespread under-estimation by older people of their own mental abilities – 'I'm too old to learn that!' But in a number of places new experimental programmes have been run in mental fitness, or mental aerobics, that demonstrate that not only can people engage in considerable intellectual activity as they age, but that it can both slow down the decline in their mental functioning and also improve it.

Cusack and Thompson (1998) report on a project initiated in one older people's centre that has been ongoing in Vancouver. It consists of a six-week needs assessment programme and eight-week research programme of workshops. The programme consisted of:

- games and puzzles;
- discussion and critical thinking;
- helping participants develop a positive mental attitude;
- helping them to speak out about what they were learning;
- doing homework;
- being given tips about how to remember.

The outcome was that there was an increase in the measured scores for: creativity, optimism, openness to new ideas, willingness to take risks, mental flexibility, willingness to speak their minds, ability to learn new things, memory and confidence that they can remember. The authors also state that the change in the nature of the language of the participants was dramatic and, overall, there was an increase in mental fitness. Cusack and Thompson (1998, p 315) report one of the participants saying: 'I have found a new-found energy that is enabling me to think more clearly. I am doing things I never thought I could because of this excitement I have. Perhaps it was the limiting beliefs that held me back.' Another participant said that everybody in the family now says, 'Ask Grandma, she remembers everything' and another saying that her niece told her that she wanted to emulate her when she grows up because she is always 'busy doing new and exciting things' (Cusack and Thompson, 1998, p 315).

A similar approach has been adopted in Texas in mental aerobics in which classes are held in a residential centre and in a senior centre. Participants engage each week in spontaneous mental drill, a quiz, verbal puzzles, a maths problem and a spatial or logic problem. Paggi and Hayslip (1999) report that the participants found that it keeps their minds active, they enjoy socializing and the challenge they face is fun. In a less formal way, it is possible for anybody to purchase books on puzzles, do crossword puzzles, and generally engage in exercises to stretch the mind – it is having the mental discipline to do it. Of course, regular reading and tackling difficult topics in that reading is also part of the same process. Cusack and Thompson (1998, p 315) conclude that: 'A mental fitness course is not a self-indulgent luxury for seniors – it is a critical component for healthy ageing and it is foundational to meaningful intergenerational dialogue and exchange.'

Empowering older adults

Throughout this chapter, there is an underlying theme that once older adults feel free to engage in critical thought, they are empowered. The concept of empowerment, however, has often been associated with radical adult education but it is used here to refer to the idea that individuals are taught that they are free and able to challenge the views being put forward by those in authority because they have the life experience, skills and talents to play a significant role in whatever process they are involved. They also have the space and freedom to take responsibility for their own actions as a result of their own informed and independent or shared decisions.

The empowerers may be teachers, carers or administrators. Some of the teaching approaches mentioned in Chapter 4 empower learners whilst others disempower them. Similarly, carers and administrators of care can either empower of disempower those who are in their care by the way that they care for them. Even in business and industry, this is becoming recognized as a truism. Goleman (1998, p 126) writes: 'Bosses who micro-manage – who take control over small details best left to subordinates – may *seem* to have the initiative, but they lack the basic awareness of how their actions affect other people. Initiative without empathy – or a sense of the bigger picture – can be destructive and typifies managers who perform badly.' [Italics in the original.] Considerable research has been undertaken in this area – most of which illustrates quite clearly that those older adults who learn that they are empowered demonstrate a much richer lifestyle and even live longer.

There is a sense in which the above discussion raises considerable questions about the concepts of care and rehabilitation. A number of nurses have implied to me that they view rehabilitation as the time when they do things for the patients so that they can get them back to normal life, and the things that they do seem to be mostly physical. In precisely the same way, care is often seen as doing things for the older person or the patient, rather than empowering the patients or the older persons to do it for themselves. We have probably all witnessed this in residential homes and in rehabilitation hospital wards. In a sense, there is often an unrecognized disempowerment or dependency-creation – often out of the kindest of motives – in some of these activities.

Among the many research reports about the way that older adults can be empowered, a significant one by Strom *et al* (1997, pp 588–89) refers back to work reported by Rodin and Langer (1977). The ethics of the research that they report might now be considered debatable but the 91 residents in a Connecticut residential home were divided into two groups. One group was told that the institution expected them to be responsible for several everyday type decisions around the nursing home whereas the others were told that the staff had this responsibility and also had the commitment to take care of them. Within a few weeks it was clear that the first group had greater happiness, enjoyed more interpersonal contacts, showed higher levels of mental alertness and, within 18 months the death rate in this group had dropped to 15 per cent. It was normally 25 per cent. By contrast, 71 per cent of the latter group had deteriorated within a few weeks and the death rate had increased to 30 per cent. Similar results were reported by Johnson (1993) in the United Kingdom when she compared two precisely similar residential homes run by the same local authority but having different care regimes, although she did not examine death rates. She points out that the one which empowered the residents actually required little over half the amount of staff which is also clearly financially advantageous – although she rightly acknowledges that the level of staffing should not be determined by finances but by the needs of the residents.

The Continuum Center of Oakland University in Michigan has developed a number of empowering workshops for older people, such as 'Take Charge of Your Own Aging', 'Personal Growth for Older Adults' and 'Growing Older and Bolder'. Such programmes help older adults improve their interpersonal communication skills and also to express their feelings and many of the participants are pleasantly surprised that they can learn to express themselves better at their age (Waters and Goodman, 1990, p 191).

Cusack (1999) also argues that seniors can and should be empowered so that they can take leadership roles, as many that actually work on behalf of seniors do not always appreciate the richness of the experience of the elders. Significantly, in the leadership training programme that she describes, the shared servant-leader role is one appreciated by the seniors. In undertaking leadership training, one of the participants reports that he changed from authoritarian to shared servant-leadership, increased in self-confidence and willingness to accept responsibility, and also became more observant and better able to communicate with others. Cusack (1999) argues that this form of empowerment should be a central focus for the education of older adults.

In contrast, Stone (1992, pp 92–105) shows from his research into day care centres in Stepney that they operate 'with the convenience of the provider frequently taking precedence over consumer needs' (p 92), and that the feeling that the way they function to disempower clients is because they are designed by able-bodied adults. This is clearly the traditional management model but one which is inappropriate for the needs of clients.

This generates a classic dilemma, however, because if elderly frail people are empowered and retain a degree of autonomy, they may occasionally harm themselves, and then the carers are criticized for not having been professional enough, etc. Yet if they offer 'too much' care, they may remove the older person's autonomy which might result in long term deleterious consequences.

Conclusion

If we think back to the learning model that we discussed in Chapter 2, we can see that learning is integrally linked to the person's biography. We do not teach new skills or old skills, neither do we teach new knowledge or older knowledge – we teach people new knowledge and skills, and so on. Additionally, we offer our help as teachers so that the learners can learn and become independent of us; so that the learners can become empowered. At the heart of this discussion, then, is respect for the personhood of the other. As we have seen, through the process of learning the older participants have gained more quality in their lives; they have new attitudes, new beliefs and even new values. Learning, and especially learning in relationship, is one of the major driving forces of humanity. The more we learn, the more we grow and develop and continue to do so – even into later life.

In common with people of all ages, if we are given space we can utilize our learning and then learn new things and continue to grow and develop. We can become empowered. However, we can sometimes be denied this space and disempowered inadvertently, even by well-meaning and loving adults who seek to care for us. Herein lies a major problem that exists because the significance of learning in our lives is not fully or widely recognized.

Those who work with older adults should all learn the importance of learning to living itself and should seek to enable all adults, whatever their age and in whatever situation they are in, to be learners. Carers and educators of the elderly should understand the significance of learning and see the significance of becoming learning therapists as part of their everyday role. Workers with the elderly should see this as an important part of their role but, unfortunately, many of them concentrate only on physical care and occasionally on entertaining those for whom we care, both of which are necessary aspects of care, but by no means constitute its totality.

When I have discussed the idea of the learning therapist with other therapists and carers, they have all said that this is part of the role of the physiotherapist, part of the role of the occupational therapist, part of the role of the nurse – and so it is. But we need to see the major significance of learning and to place it at the heart of care itself. Consequently, it is essential to generate specialist carers who understand all aspects of learning and who are prepared to organize learning exercises and therapy for all those who come to day centres, who live in residential care and those who are patients in hospitals.

11

Learning in the fourth age

Most current academic research in educational gerontology focuses on the third age. This may be because it has been necessary for society to adjust to having a large physically and mentally active retired population for the first time. However, more people than ever before are living to be much older, and while some at 75 years old are still physically and mentally active, by this age others have begun to lose their physical health, their mental health, or both. Naturally, we have to recognize that by this age, the desire to learn new things and to face more obstacles sometimes deserts people and there is a sense in which this may be a natural aspect in reaching very old age. However, for some, there is still the desire to learn new things, and for most people a great deal of incidental learning still occurs. Indeed, it is also a time when reduced physical activity means that people might spend more time reflecting upon their lives and contemplating their own self. This is also a period of life about which we do not know sufficient – about how and what people want to learn or do – since research about learning amongst the old–old is still very limited. Indeed, until recently, many have just been cared for physically, with little reference to their mental activities – images of the elderly sitting in chairs positioned around the walls of large rooms in residential homes, doing nothing and being left to their own thoughts are commonplace. It was the best form of caring that we knew in the past: people were safe, had somewhere to live, were fed and looked after. It is for this reason that we focused on the learning therapist in the last chapter since caring also involves caring about the mental fitness of the elderly as well as their physical well-being.

In this brief chapter we shall look at learning opportunities for the physically disabled and we shall then begin to explore the idea of life history and reminiscence, confusion and dementia and, finally, we shall look briefly at the last stages of life.

Learning for the physically disabled

Physical disability is not age-related and so public buildings, such as adult education centres, should have the necessary facilities to enable older adult learners to attend programmes, and so on. However, there are now opportunities for face-to-face education to take place in residential homes, since Universities of the Third Age have programmed some of their courses in these homes for those who want them and if the residential care home management will allow it. It does appear, however, that some of these courses have floundered a little since it has been difficult to maintain numbers and interest.

Additionally, distance education has made it possible for older people to study with the Open University. Older people may wish to register for a whole degree course but it is possible to enrol for individual modules and study at home, or in residential care, with tutor support. Many other educational institutions now offer education courses at a distance and so older, physically disabled people need not feel completely denied these formal learning opportunities. Moreover, with the introduction of the World Wide Web, opportunities to learn are even greater than ever before. As older people gain confidence with the use of personal computers (and as we have already pointed out, learning to use personal computers is one of the most popular adult education courses amongst the elderly) they can plug into the Web and download material, learn from a wide variety of sources and keep in touch with all their areas of interest. Indeed, day care centres might actually install personal computers and encourage some of the people who participate in their activities to use them. Residential care homes should have facilities in all rooms for residents to install their own computing equipment, and so on. Not only does this facilitate learning, it enables older people to maintain contact with more of their friends around the world through electronic mail and also to prevent their horizons from narrowing to their own small residential world. Residential homes themselves might have their own programmes with personal computers, such as 'twinning' with other homes in this country and abroad, so that they help to maintain a lively interest amongst their own residents in the world around them and, indeed, with each other.

However, face-to-face learning is still very important for some groups of people, especially for those who live alone. Nick Osmond (1995) has conducted a very interesting project at a stroke rehabilitation centre in Brighton. He convened a group of stroke victims who, naturally, wished to talk about their experiences. The group decided to write a book about themselves and the meetings became quite central to their lives. They were able to discuss their experiences, which were tape-recorded, wrote about them and then were edited into a book that was marketed. Osmond undertook a second similar project with carers. He (1995, p 181) points out that both groups were very lively, therapeutic and empowering. He (1995, p 182) suggests that:

> The learning that went on... was more about people disclosing their
> own experience and discovering one another's than learning about
> writing skills. By articulating, and hearing others articulate, a particular
> experience, and by focusing on a common difficulty or shared pain, it
> was as though the experience took on some sort of validity. It was there,
> outside, and that somehow made it easier to deal with. The writing was
> a by-product and yet, precisely because we were not focusing on the
> skills of writing but on communication as an end product, it seems to
> come out as a quite adequate expression of what people had to say.

In this sense, their learning was by doing, and we will recall that this is one of the
paths in the learning diagram that we expounded in Chapter 2. Furthermore, the
common difficulty and the shared pain were easier to withstand when in relationship with others. Osmond also points out that the meeting for both the books
enabled a bonding to take place between the participants and so, in future
projects, he maintains that plans should be made for continuing the group meetings after the project has been completed.

Other similar programmes for the very elderly include assertiveness training.
Corby (1975) reported that, after a programme of four one-hour assertiveness
sessions with a group of very old people (average age 86 years) in an American
retirement home, the participants increased their personal disclosure levels by 67
per cent (cited in Waters and Goodman, 1990, p 190).

Empowering residents to run their own programmes through residents'
committees and so on, might help overcome some of the problems that occur in
residential homes, especially as older people come into these homes with a wide
range of abilities and expertise. It is so easy for the workers in the home to
misjudge what might be of interest to residents. For instance, I recently heard of
one elderly person asking the warden of a residential home what type of musical
programme the home provided for its residents. The warden replied that 'they
had someone to come in and play the old tunes on the piano occasionally because
they like that', but when that person then asked one of the residents who was her
favourite composer, she got the response 'Chopin'! That resident might have
been in the minority for that home, but if the residents themselves were involved
in suggesting and preparing their own programmes, such anomalies might be
avoided. Nevertheless, there is value in hearing and singing the old tunes since it
does aid memory recall and stimulates community participation.

Life history and reminiscence

In the learning diagram in Chapter 2, it will be recalled that there is a dotted line
back from memorization to experience. We all undergo this learning process of
recalling our memories and reinterpreting them in the light of our current biog-

raphy and the new social situation in which we find ourselves. In this we construct, or reconstruct, our experiences and this is the nature of autobiography. Peter Alheit (1995, p 57) cites Kirkegaard: 'Life can only be understood backwards. In the meantime, it has to be lived forwards', but as we get towards the end of our lives our forward time perspective shortens and we might tend to look backwards more often. Older people write their life stories for the sake of their grandchildren. Life history and reminiscence appear to play a larger role in our lives. Indeed, it enables us to reach back into our being itself, as we pointed out in Chapter 3, and reconstruct our learning and living.

In this sense, life history may be seen as a form of oral history, something of a new discipline in the United Kingdom until the late 1960s, although it was also taking its place in the psychology of old age about the same time. In the United Kingdom, *Help the Aged's* tape/slide programme *Recall* was a major influence in relating oral history to older people, although reminiscence work was already well established in the United States. Merriam (1985), for instance, cites research from Cameron (1972) that suggested that people of all ages reminisce and that older people do not look back to the more distant past more frequently than do younger people. Merriam cites four major functions of reminiscence:

- life satisfaction;
- adaptation to stress;
- cognitive functioning;
- ego integrity.

The more that people reminisce about the positive things of their lives the more likely they are to be satisfied with it. Indeed, reminiscing as an enjoyable activity increases life satisfaction, but the reverse is also true (Merriam and Cross, 1981). Being aware of the content of older people's reminiscing can, therefore, make us aware of the satisfaction older people have with their lives. Having reviewed several studies of reminiscence, Merriam (1985, p 57) concluded that: '... reminiscence functions as an adaptive mechanism or facilitates personality reorganization in late adulthood. Reminiscence appears to play a role in life satisfaction, coping with stress, enhancing cognitive functioning and facilitating the life review process.' She pointed out that research in this area is still sparse. Since she wrote, however, there has been considerable research on dementia and reminiscence. Gibson (1995, p 4) suggested that:

> reminiscence is one way of pushing back or holding at bay, at least for a time, this shrinking world (of a person suffering from dementia). We all possess memories, we all have our own unique life history that, for good or ill, however it has turned out, is an indissoluble part of ourselves, our own unique personhood. This recall takes place in the present. It is a here and now process which holds the teller and the told in relationship

with each other. People with dementia can be helped to hang on to their past and by sharing it with others, enrich present associations, enlarge sympathies, and provide clues about how they would like their present life and living arrangements to be ordered. Reminiscence is a way of providing opportunities for people with dementia to bear witness to their lives, whether they be long or short, satisfactory or unsatisfactory.

Merriam (1985) suggested four reasons why there should be educational intervention in order to facilitate reminiscence:

- It might lead to a better old age.
- It appears to be a therapeutic activity.
- It is a good way for professionals to get to know their clients.
- It is a good resource to help older people to continue their learning.

Significantly, she omitted the discussion raised by Gibson about the need for people to present themselves to others with as much of the fullness of their identity as they can. Of her other points, the first two and the final points have already been discussed in this book and so we look to the third. While there is a lot of research that supports the relationship between professionals knowing their patients and caring and it seems both natural and important, research by Hillman *et al* (1999, pp 37–49) has called it into question. Their research does seem to contradict a lot of the previous research findings by suggesting that knowing the life histories of patients does not help care staff. They point out, however, that the relationship between care staff and patients had already been created before the former learnt about the life histories of the people for whom they were caring, and so when they were told the background during the research it made little difference to the way that they thought about those for whom they were supposed to care. The staff still did not like those 'more difficult people' for whom they cared. Clearly, in the situation described in the research, there was not always a satisfactory relationship between the older residents and the care staff, and this might account for the research findings. I am not sure that their research questions the need for professionals to understand the background of those being cared for, as much as it reports on the need for good and understanding relationships to be created from the outset. This involves the care staff getting to know and understand their residents. It is necessary to begin a care relationship with an understanding of the life history of the patient, but even more – with the intention of entering a genuine personal relationship with a person for whom one can genuinely care.

One significant indication of the need to know the patient is recorded in the beautiful poem 'Kate' published by Carver and Lilliard (1978, pp ix–x). Kate was an old woman who lived in a hospital and did not speak but occasionally she was seen to write something. After her death a beautiful poem which she had written about her experience and her life was found in her locker. The poem is a protest, a cry for the need for a genuine relationship with the nurses and a sign that older people need to be enabled to express what goes on in their minds, even when they are physically disabled. This is a beautiful but poignant reminiscence. What a tragedy and what a loss that she was left to pen the words:

> What do you see nurse
> What do you see?
> Are you thinking
> when you are looking at me
> A crabbit old woman
> Not very wise.

> So open your eyes nurses,
> Open and see,
> Not a crabbit old woman,
> Look closer – see ME.

The poem is 88 lines long and in the middle there is her life story, but the opening and closing lines tell another story. Unfortunately she had learnt through all the experiences of every day that nobody had the time to help her communicate and she learnt that she was treated as a non-person. This is the incidental learning that we all experience, but since most of us also learn through other means we are less aware of the significance of incidental learning. Yet this incidental learning is one of the confused person's main ways of knowing, and it is one that carers of the very sick and mentally frail should be aware of, so that through their care they communicate both an awareness of the personhood of the other but also that they have the time to communicate with them. This will not happen if the traditional professional ethic of carers remains and they keep their distance between themselves and their patients. Clearly the impersonal professional ethic itself is questionable and carers have to be prepared to enter personal relationships. They have to be prepared to laugh with those for whom they care when they are happy and cry with them when they are down. The care relationship must be a person-centred one.

Significantly, in my own experience of working with older people, reminiscence enables them to reclaim their lives. This is something that Pineau (1995, p 44) also discovered. It helps older people to gain ego integrity. Now some retirement homes have reminiscence rooms, decorated in the style of an earlier period in order to stimulate recall, and workers are trained in reminiscence work (Kirkwood, 1987). Kitwood (1997, p 56) cites Sutton's (1995) PhD thesis in which she argues that reminiscence is not merely a matter of factual recall but a form of interpersonal communication. Reminiscence may help older people both to say 'This is me!' but also to achieve a state of integrity, which Erikson (1950, p 260) describes thus:

> Although aware of the relativity of all the various lifestyles which have given meaning to human striving, the possessor of integrity is ready to defend the dignity of his own style against all physical and economic threats. For he knows that an individual life is the accidental coincidence of but one life cycle with but one segment of history; and that for him all human integrity stands or falls with the one style of integrity of which he partakes. The style of integrity developed by his culture or civilization thus becomes the 'patrimony of the soul', the seal of his moral paternity of himself.

By contrast, people who are filled with despair know that there is no time to start again and to find another way to achieve integrity. For those in despair, there is a need for friendship, counselling or even for discussing with clergy and lay people from their own religious background about their needs. Through reminiscence and other forms of counselling they may be helped to achieve a better psychological state. It is no accident that the above passage from Erikson reflects the language of spirituality − for here we find the heart of our humanity, of our existence itself. Learning, as we argued in Chapter 3, is ultimately about being.

Learning in confusion and dementia

Confusion is different from dementia and may be defined as 'thinking with less than accustomed clarity' (Bryne, 1995, p 2, cited from McIsaac, 1996, p 44). McIsaac, adopting an interactionist perspective, makes the basic point that older people have had a lifetime of learning how to communicate and that even in their confusion they may not have lost that skill − some may have lost more of it than others. However, they may find it difficult to respond quickly or in normal ways, so that other people need to learn how to receive their communication. People need more time to be with people and learn the language and communication processes of the confused.

Because they may seek to communicate in different ways and are often not understood, the confused run the danger of being stereotyped as not being able to communicate at all. McIsaac (1996, p 52) records a situation from his own research. An elderly person, asked about what she thought about the activity going on in the room, replied: 'Nobody ever asked me that before… I don't pay much attention. I can't be bothered − I suppose I'm just not interested in anything much… I sit here − well… you have to… it's what we do.'

The same person was described by the staff as 'sweet, no trouble, quiet' and 'really not here at all'! The old lady had learnt that she just had to sit there and do nothing, but the staff treated her as confused and no trouble and so she became more inactive. As far as the staff were concerned she was sweet and quiet – effectively a non-person. Perhaps we have all got to learn that to empower people to be persons means that we should expect them to impinge upon us and our desires. In other words, they should be a trouble because this is the nature of relationship and of care.

But confused people can learn to do things again and gain a degree of independence, provided that the teachers are loving, caring and skilled. I have personally witnessed an elderly woman, confused because she had been in a rehabilitation hospital for two months, during which time she received little mental stimulation but good physical care, being taught to live alone and to do basic things for herself when she returned to her sheltered accommodation. She was empowered by being exposed to basic infant teaching methods employed in a loving and caring adult manner by a very skilled teacher/carer – a learning therapist. The older woman learnt once again that she could do things and that she could actually be independent to some degree. But the communication was often difficult and every moment was a learning experience for everybody involved. Wilson (1999, p 106) also shows that a person with dementia, whom he calls Barbara, had her own activity table and she was able to spend an hour a time at the table doing things. She was also able to communicate because she was in a situation in which she was loved and treasured as a person. As McIsaac argues (1996, pp 53–54): 'a more sensitive approach to communication with older people in a confused state can reveal their thoughts and feelings which paint quite a different picture from what may be initially perceived by others. To recognize the confused older person as 'active' rather than 'passive' provides the individual with the opportunity to maintain identity in social situations despite any impairment.'

There is also evidence to suggest that the incidence of depression is high in residential care and, as Murphy (1993) points out, a period of depression is one in which old people often lose friendships and family contact because of the nature of their illness. This merely exacerbates their condition. It is a time when the depressed need to know that they are valued persons but it is often one in which they are denied opportunity to reminisce and to relate to others.

Perhaps the most research in this area has been conducted on people suffering from Alzheimer's disease. In a very brave autobiographical account of suffering from the disease in which he helps others to learn about it, Robert Davies tells of the things that he learnt as he experienced the disease to help him to retain maximum control and peace of mind:

- the importance of familiar routines as a way of reducing demands;
- the continual battle against paranoid beliefs;
- the fear of making mistakes that will be punished by further losses of freedom;
- the panic and exhaustion brought on by disorientation in place;

- difficulty in focusing attention;
- inability to see spacial relationships between objects;
- difficulty in recalling some of the past, but good recognition of long term memory prompts;
- the effectiveness of physical exercise at times of mental 'darkness and emptiness';
- finding new ways to communicate, such as the use of a word processor;
- use of tape recorded books of a long-time favourite author to help him get to sleep;
- the simple desire for friendship and acceptance from others;
- the need to give up certain areas of responsibility and allow someone else to care for him. (Summary taken from Arigho, 1995, p 17.)

It is significant that Davies's book tells us how important is the familiar, so that he can do things without having to think too much about them, how much the physical aspect is important for his mental well-being and just how important is his relationship with others who accept him for who he is. He has to live in a world in which he can trust others. Kitwood (1997) also points out that the combination of gradually advancing failure of mental powers plus changes in the pattern of social relationships are both associated with the onset of dementia. He focuses on the relationship between those who suffer the disease and the carers, but he also records a variety of new ways of caring for people with dementia, including enabling them to live in sheltered accommodation and so on, so that they can still be occupied and feel that they have power over their lives. He (1997, p 99) writes: 'Personhood must be continually replenished; if it is not, relational confidence and good feeling will drain away, leaving a person with a subjective world that is again in chaos and ruin.'

In other words, through the interpersonal relationships between those with dementia and their carers, those who are suffering have still to keep on learning that their personhood is valued, that *they* are valued and that they can still have some power over their own lives. Otherwise, they may learn to become totally disinterested in what is going on around them because they learn incidentally that others no longer consider them important.

Kitwood (1997), and others who write about care, focuses upon person-centred care. It is a telling phrase and it does communicate the importance of personhood but it still runs the risk of losing the other central plank in caring – the relationship. Perhaps relationship-centred care might be an even more significant term.

The last stages of life

Most of the research on death and dying in education has been about the professional continuing education of the carers (see, for instance, Hawkett, 1988; Allen, Darby and Fee, 1990) and about the process of care itself. Even here the significance of the interactive approach is emphasized. Cicely Saunders (1978, p 416) says that caring for the dying is a shared work. In contrast, Wilcock (1999, pp 78–81) tells of the lonely death of an old lady, alone and almost uncared for, as the death that most haunts her. Even in the last stages of life, however, individuals do need relationship and may still seek answers to their questions of meaning. Hawkett (1988, p 9) wrote:

> Many patients in their own way try to make sense out of what is happening. This requires a carer who is sensitive and alert. Staying with someone who is facing death when there are no answers and no way of taking away the approaching pain of separation is hard. Allowing the patient to express anger and guilt, and not being defensive or withdrawing is an important aspect of caring. When the patient has the freedom to ask 'why' then the emotional and spiritual aspects of total pain are being addressed.

Answers may be forthcoming and these may offer support and comfort at this difficult time. There are few people who have made death a learning experience, but one who did was Morrie Schwartz (Albom, 1997), a sociology professor in America who, when he knew he was dying decided to make the record of his dying a human textbook: *Study me in my slow and painful demise. Watch what happens to me. Learn with me* (Albom, 1997, p 10). Surrounded by loving carers, Morrie Schwartz bravely recorded the process of dying and this book, written by one of his former students, records some of the lessons he learnt during the process of dying from the incurable Lou Gehrig's disease (amyotrophic lateral sclerosis). What follows perhaps reflects those words from Voltaire, 'The heart does not age, but it is sad having to house it in ruins' (cited from Nielsen and Thyssen, 1993, p 17). Those lessons began when he asked the former student, then a well-known journalist about himself:

- What was he giving to the community?
- Was he at peace with himself?
- Was he trying to be as human as he could be?

Albom records what he learnt as the weeks went by but he also records what the dying person considered important lessons to be learnt by everyone:

- The most important thing in life is to learn how to give out love, and to let it come in (p 52; pp 127–28).
- Love is the only rational act (p 52).
- Morrie wanted to share his life (pp 62–63).

- We all need teachers in our lives to make us think about these things because our culture does not encourage us to do this (pp 64–65).
- When friends visit his emotions are high – but he had depressions, worrying about the gradual loss of his body, especially his voice. The only way he could give to others when his voice failed would be by getting them to ask him 'yes' or 'no' questions (pp 70–71).
- It is important to share emotion and to touch each other (pp 70–71; p 128).
- Everybody knows that they are going to die – but nobody believes it. If they did they would do things differently (p 81).
- Once you learn how to die, you learn how to live (pp 82–83).
- Love each other or we perish (pp 91–92; p 149).
- Do not cling to things because everything is impermanent (p 103).
- Learn to enjoy dependency when you can no longer be independent (p 116).
- It is impossible for the old not to envy the young, but learn to accept who you are and revel in it (pp 119–21).
- We all need people (p 157).
- Invest in the human family (p 157).
- Death ends a life, not a relationship (p 174).

In a sense, this study is not so much learning about dying but learning what a dying professor wants to say to the world about the lessons that he has learnt. It is a form of reminiscence – but perhaps it is more. We can learn about the fact that even in the most extreme circumstances, provided that there are good relationships, we can still retain our humanity.

Martin Buber (1959, p 18) wrote that in the beginning is relation and without relationship there can be no 'I' – no personal identity. In relationship persons become persons and it is clear from the above that Morrie Schwartz was enabled to be a person, a learner and a teacher, until he died. Schwartz was an exceptional man, but it still required courage and strength to face what he did and to share his pain, suffering and the lessons about living that he learnt. But without the human relationships, people who cared for him, his lessons might never have been learnt and they might never have been communicated for others to learn.

Conclusion

Lifelong learning really is lifelong. But perhaps not everybody is able to learn the lessons from life quite so easily as did Morrie Schwartz nor communicate them in quite such an articulate but emotionally moving manner. Robert Davies likewise tells us what he was learning as his Alzheimer's disease progressed. But Kate might also have had many things to tell us about her learning had the people who surrounded her enabled her to enter similar relationships. Much has been written about learning during the first stages of life, little about the final stages and so more research and understanding is necessary. Perhaps, as significantly, we have seen how important is the carer to the process of learning. Learning is not just about education, it is about health care and about living itself. As we pointed out earlier, learning is a driving force in life itself and we continue to learn through all the different ways that we discussed earlier in this book – both deliberately and incidentally. Understanding this process is not something restricted to an academic discipline or to an educational practice – learning transcends all disciplines and practices – carers are teachers, teachers are (or should be) carers. Contemplation, reminiscence and those forms of learning about which behaviourism could tell us little are as significant to our being as are those more instrumental forms of learning that are espoused by modern educational policy.

For as long as we have our faculties, and this appears to be far longer than generally assumed, we are able to learn. We learn from every situation in which we find ourselves and from whomever we meet. But some of those situations might be made richer and more orientated to helping older people learn and interact with their environment. And some of those individuals with whom we interact need to understand a little more that whether they intend it or otherwise they are people from whom we learn. Leaving aside all the physical and mental health aspects of caring, it is perhaps necessary for professionals to understand the issues that we have touched upon in this book and its final chapter we examine the need to learn to work with older people.

12

Learning to work with elders

This book is about the significance of learning in the lives of elderly people – both planned and incidental learning. It has been suggested that learning is crucial to all aspects of personal and social living, to both mental and physical life, and to both the length and quality of life itself. In other words, learning is fundamental to human being. What we have been examining is, literally, lifelong learning at the latter end of life. But it is not always the type of planned learning that is associated with education and classrooms – often it is unplanned and incidental. However, what we have seen is something that every educator of adults, every therapist and every carer – whether professional or voluntary – should understand – that learning is itself a driving force of life itself. Everybody who works with older learners can be a learning therapist. Since learning is a human process that covers every aspect of human living, those who should be aware of the significance of learning cover all the professions and occupations who work with the elderly. Learning therapy is both educative and therapeutic – it is about caring for and developing the learners whether they are students or frail elderly in need of nursing and medical care.

Consequently, in this brief final chapter we will look at some of the essential aspects of older people's learning that everyone who works with the elderly should know. This is not a curriculum for the professional preparation of people who work with the elderly; it is much more a programme that might be included in their continuing professional education. With few exceptions, eg Kirkwood (1987), most of the research undertaken about the education and training of educators and care staff working with elders is about their initial professional preparation in order to undertake the work rather than their continuing professional education, or about courses for volunteers.

We recognize that staff from the established professions who work with elders, eg education, medicine, nursing, occupational therapy and physiotherapy etc, will probably have all undertaken their speciality relating to the elderly, where it exists, in their professional preparation. But the extent to which they will have studied the significance of learning in the lives of the elderly is much more questionable. In addition, there are many untrained care staff in residential homes and, despite courses like the ones run by the Royal Institute for Public Heath and Hygiene, many of them remain untrained. Indeed, the owners of many of these homes are most likely to continue to employ untrained staff since it keeps the costs down (and I recognize that if the costs of care are kept low then this can be beneficial to poorer people as well as to the owners). Nevertheless, despite the excellent physical care that many of these carers provide, the lack of training can do a great deal of mental harm to the people for whom they care. Consequently, failure to look at the place of learning and mental fitness among all that work with the elderly, especially the frail elderly, can be detrimental to the older people's well-being.

Firstly, we want to argue that in this learning society there should be a new specialist – the learning therapist. Secondly, we want to advocate a continuing education programme about learning in later life that should be undertaken by all educators and carers of the elderly, whether this is their professional specialism or not. In precisely the same way as residential homes are registered, so there should be some regulatory mechanism to ensure that all those who work with the elderly are undertaking regular continuing education courses. In addition, we want to argue that teaching older people not only about educational opportunities but also about the benefits of self-help and self-directed learning should also form at least a part of pre-retirement education.

This chapter is divided into four sections. Firstly, learning about learning; secondly, creating a learning environment for the elderly; thirdly, understanding the role of a learning therapist and professional training; fourthly, understanding the morality of the relationship between the older person and the worker. Finally, there is a brief conclusion that reverts back to the introductory chapter and to the way that recognition of the significance of learning for older people has gradually emerged during the twentieth century.

Learning about learning

Many aspects of teaching and care can only be learnt by practice, as Clark (1999) has shown by introducing service-learning education for workers with the elderly. But it is also necessary to understand something about the learning process and this is perhaps better undertaken in continuing professional education sessions – even in post-graduate taught Masters degrees for those who do not have training in the education of adults.

A great deal of the research that has been undertaken into learning has been done with animals and small children, which is far removed from the lives of the old and the very old. However, the piece of research that I undertook into adult learning was about adults learning, and was fully reported in Chapter 2. It is upon that model that much of this book has been based and it is one which has been used in a module of a taught Masters programme for those working with the third and fourth age. The relevance of the model was recognized and the programme itself was regarded as relevant to the work of the interdisciplinary group of students – nurses, occupational therapists, physiotherapists and care home managers. The theory of that course is covered in the early chapters of this book. However, it is important to understand the learning processes themselves, to recognize both their planned and incidental nature and also to recognize the three different contexts within which all forms of learning occur. Much more significantly, however, it is necessary to understand that the relationship between learning and the learner's biography constitutes a fundamental part of our understanding about learning.

In a great deal of literature, especially policy literature, learning is regarded as something instrumental. Even in the literature about learning, with dogs, pigeons, rats and even young children, the process is instrumental. Teaching is traditionally an instrumental process and the learners learn what they are taught. Here the learning process apparently ends since the aims of the teaching have been fulfilled. Behaviourism is predicated on the achievement of measurable end products. The only trouble with learning is that this apparently measurable end product is not the actual end product. It is not the content learnt that is the end product, but the effect that the learning has on the learners themselves. We do not teach skills, or mathematics, and so on – we teach people skills, mathematics, etc. We have to put the persons back into the process. All learning is incorporated into the learners' biography and this is not measurable. This is also recognized by the biographical approach in adult education (Alheit *et al* 1995) to which reference was made earlier.

At the same time, the content is important and this should not be downplayed in any way. Indeed, it is necessary to recognize that older people are still able to participate in educational courses, even very advanced ones, and can still be developing intellectually. It is not necessary to simplify material, although it may be necessary to change the approaches to and the techniques of the teaching.

However, the learning that is incorporated into our biographies is not always to do with that which we were taught instrumentally, it is often the learning that occurs outside of the educational framework, incidentally and in an unplanned way (boxes D–F in Figure 2.2 in Chapter 2). But a great deal of our learning does not require a teacher. Our ways of knowing are many and varied as the feminist literature has demonstrated (see, for instance, Belenky *et al* 1986). Every time we learn our biographies are changed (as are our synapses) and at different times in our lives we recall these memories. Some of the unpleasant learning experiences are repressed or suppressed but may still affect our behaviour without our being aware of it.

Towards the end of our lives all of the learning that has affected our being appears in some way to be self-assessed and those who work with the elderly both have to understand that older people are still learning incidentally and at the same time they are sometimes trying to reclaim their lives by reframing their previous learning experiences through reflection and reminiscence.

It is, therefore, necessary for those who work with the elderly to be aware of both the processes and the functions of learning in the human biography and to put these more instrumental approaches into perspective. Learning is not merely lifelong – it is lifetime and lifewide; it is about life itself. Being aware of the learning processes is a necessary reason for changing our approaches to teaching and caring for the elderly. We shall, however, return to this in the fourth section of this chapter.

Creating a learning environment

Go into any good school and around the walls there will be pictures, diagrams, examples of the children's learning. It is impossible to escape from the feeling that the school is a place where learning is taking place. This is also true for most adult education institutes. It is a learning environment. A common picture in a residential home or a rehabilitation hospital, in contrast, is for elderly people to be sitting around the sides of a room in comfortable chairs or to be lying in beds with little or no mental stimulation. Now, it has to be recognized that there are many people who do not necessarily want to be stimulated, especially not in the same way as children in a school! Nevertheless, the fact that they receive little or no mental stimulation might be one, among many reasons, why some people become confused. They also learn that they are not expected to be interested in things – as the lady reported by McIsaac in the previous chapter said. It is necessary, therefore, to create an atmosphere and an environment in which it is not only possible to continue learning, but that older people regard it as something that is not exceptional, but, rather that they are *expected* to be interested in things. There should be a sub-culture orientated to learning. This does not mean, however, that the carers have got to see themselves as teachers so much as all who work with the elderly should be facilitators of learning opportunities. There should be:

● games and puzzles, playing cards, books and newspapers, and so on, widely available;
● regular sessions where those who are able are invited to participate in both physical and mental aerobics;
● more opportunities for discussion about daily events seen on the television or read about in the newspapers, not only amongst themselves but with others who come and visit;
● computers made available;

- more opportunities to do things around the place of residence, whether it be a rehabilitation ward in a hospital or a residential home.

In the same way, the care staff should encourage this in both a formal and informal manner, even if they do little more than encourage conversation between themselves and the residents, and between the residents themselves.

Furthermore, residential homes might provide workrooms so that older residents can continue their hobbies. One sheltered home known to me enabled an elderly man to retain his interest in woodwork and carpentry by making a room available to him (he had all the tools) and a space in the gardens for him to do his own gardening, both of which enriched the quality of his life in the home. Even more, it gave others something to talk to him about, so that he became a stimulant for others' interests. In addition, there should be many other stimuli provided in terms of pictures on the walls (changed regularly), music and outings, and so forth. Outings do not always have to be to exotic places. For instance, I know a group of fourth agers who love to use a coach to visit garden centres where they can look around, purchase a few presents and have tea and cakes in the restaurant. It is the stimulus, perhaps, more than the actual place that is important.

People should be encouraged to reminisce and care staff should be facilitators and listeners when this occurs. If they are busy at the time, then they should say so in a nice way but return to the person concerned at a later time and try to restart the process. Providing space for people to talk is important at this stage in people's lives.

Finally, the residents should be empowered to run their own lives, to organize things affecting their lives in the homes or wards and, in residential homes, even to have committees that make decisions and liaise with the professional staff and the managers. This might be more of a hassle for the professional staff, but the more it is, so the more they are succeeding in empowering the residents. Residents should be expected to question and to speak their minds. They should expect to know what is being done to them and why, etc. They should feel this freedom. The quiet old person dozing in a comfortable chair all day at the side of a room, apparently waking up only for meals, and complying with the requests of staff, should be regarded as a staff failure, rather than someone well cared for by the residential home staff. The way that the older people are spoken to, and about, illustrates how empowered they are. Language can be one of the most powerful weapons of control and mental abuse, but it can also be liberating and respectful.

Kitwood (1997, p 104) makes the point that research into the style and structure of 'caring organizations' for dementia sufferers has hardly been undertaken. It might be claimed here that caring organizations ought also to be learning communities and there has been little rigorous research into these in the United Kingdom, although there is a growing amount of research into some aspects of such an organization.

Learning therapists

Every worker with older adults should see their job including the work of learning therapy. This should not be hard for educators of adults, although they should be seeking more opportunities of working with the frail elderly and others who are living in residential accommodation. However, it will come as a bigger change for those who have regarded their role as mainly caring for the physical aspects of life. Yet it is a necessary change to make if the quality of life of the elderly is to be enriched.

It would be beneficial if there was one person in each hospital or residential home who was a specialist in helping create learning environments. This need not be a separate occupation, but could be a specialism learned by professionals from any of the caring professions who could then go on to conduct in-house staff training in understanding the place of learnt in the lives of the elderly. It is certainly an element that should be included in every manager's training, whether they are ward sisters or managers of residential homes, etc. The more managers recognize the importance of this aspect of care, the less we will see and hear of nurses who stop talking with patients when they see the ward manager coming in, exclaiming, 'I must get back to work now!' Care is not only physical and work is not only doing something measurable. Relating is caring and also a part of work. Helping others to learn, even incidentally, is an essential part of caring and of teaching.

The drawing together of two disparate acts 'learning' and 'caring' might seem strange in the first instance. This is partly because learning has so often been treated as something behavioural and measurable, rather that a human experiential process. It is only in recent years the educators have emphasized the human nature of learning. Additionally, the boundaries that have separated different aspects of our social living have been lowered in recent years, enabling these disparate elements to be coupled in this manner. This is a reflection of late modern society.

The moral imperative

The emphasis throughout this book has been on the personhood of the learner. It is considered essential that the link between biography and learning is never forgotten. In addition, we must not forget the fact that we learn in every walk of life, in every interaction with others, as well as when we are engaged in a self-directed learning project. Older people continue to learn in all their interactions and, significantly, in the lack of interaction that occurs, since learning is incidental and often unintended. There is, consequently, a three-way relationship between personhood, care and learning in this situation.

To the older person, lack of care or care of low quality, can deprive them of the relations to other people and the vitality which is central to the personality. The personality aspect of the care situation makes it important to relate the care discussion with the entire course of life. Being a personality means, amongst other things, to reflect on oneself and the conditions of life and to act and create one's own life. This inner mental 'work' starts in childhood and continues throughout life. (Nielsen and Thyssen, 1993, p 3.)

In caring for people, it is important to feel empathy with them as persons. Goleman (1998, pp 137–38) suggests that empathy has five elements:

- understanding others: sensing others' feelings and perspectives, and taking an active interest in their outcomes;
- service orientation: anticipating, recognizing and meeting customers' needs;
- developing others: sensing others' development and bolstering their abilities;
- leveraging diversity: cultivating opportunities through diverse people;
- political awareness: reading the social and political currents in the organization.

Obviously Goleman is writing about the work situation but, in many ways, he could also have been writing about the care situation that we are discussing. It is about respecting the personhood of others and trying to empower them. It is a situation that was discussed by Kitwood in his study of Alzheimer's disease. His (1997, p 8) definition of a person is 'a standing or status that is bestowed upon one human being, by others, in the context of a relationship and social being'. Central to his thinking, then, is that we learn about who we are in relationship with others. Kitwood (1997, pp 10–12) turned to the philosopher Martin Buber (1959) and his discussion of *I and Thou* in order to illustrate his discussion. Elsewhere (Jarvis, 1997, pp 32–36) I have summarized Buber's position, and I want to illustrate this in the following paragraphs.

People enter personal relationships through direct experience, usually because they share the same space at the same time and through so doing they have opportunity to interact with each other during which time they share a mutual bond. Before a relationship is formed, however, individuals exist in their own worlds and the Other is a stranger, who is free (Levinas, 1991, p 39) and over whom I have no power. When I and the Other are face to face, the distance between us recedes and some form of bond begins to be created. But the very formation of that bond impinges upon the freedom that is the prerogative of the Other. At the same time, my own freedom in respect to the Other is curtailed. The bond's existence, however weak, signifies that I am prepared freely to forego some freedom in order to enter a relationship. This relationship may only be for a brief period of time, although there is potentiality for it to continue beyond the first interaction, as it will in both caring and teaching relationships. Bauman (1993, p 124) suggests that:

>Moral behaviour is triggered off by the mere presence of the Other as a *face*: that is, an authority *without* force. The Other demands without *threatening* to punish, or promising rewards. The Other cannot do anything to me, neither punish nor reward: it is precisely that weakness of the Other that lays bare my strength, my ability to act, as responsibility.
>
>[Italics in original.]

I am able to enter such a relationship with the Other for whatever period of time it exists because of our common humanity. Where there is no humanity, the relationship is of necessity an I-It one. Relationships with a group, because all its members are human beings, share many of the same characteristics as with the Other, but they tend to develop the bonds of community rather than those of the more exclusive personal relationship. The exclusive personal relationship always puts at risk the community since it has the power to fragment the group. The potentiality of individual personal relationships always exists in a care or an educational situation, and this is one of the problems. Herein lies a fundamental truth: when the I-Thou relationship is formed the Stranger, or the group member, becomes a person with whom I can share a human relationship. My personhood can only be realized in relationship with another person and the Other's in relation to me. Or as Buber (1959, p 18) put it, 'In the beginning is relationship', and MacMurray (1961, p 17) suggested 'the Self is constituted by its relation to the Other'. Elsewhere, MacMurray (1961, p 24) claimed that 'the idea of an isolated Agent is self-contradictory. Any Agent is necessarily in relation to Other. Apart from this essential relationship he does not exist.' Without this relationship there can be no genuine care.

There are a number of philosophical arguments about the nature of moral good, but I do not want to explore them here. Elsewhere (Jarvis, 1997) I have done so, but in that book I argued that there is only one universal moral good. It is never wrong to be concerned for another. This is a principle – the principle of care. However, I might not have sufficient knowledge or skill to be able to do the right thing for the other, so that my practice might fall short of my principle. However, in the caring relationship alone can the one universal moral good be realized.

It is in a common humanity that the foundations of arguments for ethics is to be found and in the formation of the relationship in which personhood may be realized rests the practicalities of human existence. Indeed, Levinas (1991, p 43) argues that ethics arise when an individual's spontaneity is inhibited by the presence of Other, which is before the relationship is actually formed. Indeed, the presence of every (old) person should cause us to reconsider our own freedom and we should be willing to have our spontaneity curtailed by the presence of those for whom we care.

It will be seen from the above discussion that this position is narrow and yet

Levinas captures a great deal of the understanding of the moral relationship that is regarded here as imperative in contemporary society. He actually regards the bond that is established between the Self and the Other, the I-Thou relationship, as religion, and MacMurray develops his discussion in a similar manner in relation to the celebration of communion, although this point will not be developed further here. However, it is clear that in the potentiality of personal relationship itself lies a fundamental basis of any discussion of the nature of ethical value. MacMurray (1959, p 116) would agree with this analysis and he claimed that the 'moral rightness of an action... has its grounds in the relation of persons'. In other words, the intention to act out of concern for the Other's advantage, whatever the actual outcome, is never wrong, it is the moral ought of social living.

It is relationship, always trying to develop the personhood of the Other through providing learning opportunities for the Other, that is one major way in which care for the elderly is manifest. It is, then, a moral imperative.

Conclusion

As we pointed out at the start of this book, it has taken the better part of a century for people to recognize that adults and even older adults can actually learn. However, the conception of learning has been limited. Learning is about the whole of life, it is about the personhood of the learner and through learning we grow and develop and become the persons that we are. We often say that lifelong learning is about learning from the cradle to the grave, and that we can continue to develop until we die, and neither of these are actually rhetoric but many of the claims about lifelong learning restrict it to work and the economic dimension. We can continue to learn and develop until we die – we are always both being and in the process of becoming. Now we need a great deal more research to demonstrate the value of learning. We need to see carers trained to facilitate learning relevant to our stage or condition in life. We need to see that the facilitation of learning is part of the caring process, as well as part of the teaching one.

Learning in later life really is lifelong – it is also lifetime and lifewide learning. Learning is fundamental to our own humanity, whatever our age – it is central to life itself – and only by facilitating others' learning can we enrich their lives and demonstrate that we really care for them as persons.

References

Albom, M (1997) *Tuesdays with Morrie*, Doubleday, New York

Alheit, P (1995) Biographical learning: theoretical outline, challenges and contradictions of a new approach in adult education, in *The Biographical Approach in European Adult Education*, eds P Alheit, Bron-Wojciechowska, E Brugger and P Dominice, Verband Wiener Volksbilgung, Vienna

Allen, S, Darby, L, and Fee, R (1990) Education for death and dying, *Journal of Educational Gerontology*, **5** (1), pp 25–33

Allman, P (1984) *Self Help Learning and its Relevance for Learning and Development in Later Life in Mutual Aid Universities*, ed E Midwinter, Croom Helm, London

Annual Abstract of Statistics, HMSO, London

Anthony of Sourozh (1999) The spirituality of old age, in *Spirituality and Ageing*, ed A Jewell, Jessica Kingsley, London

Argyris, C, Putnam, R and Smith, D (1985) *Action Science*, Jossey Bass, San Francisco

Arigho, B (1995) Review of Davis R, in *Reminiscence*, 11, p 17 (published by Age Exchange, London SE3 9LA)

Arlin, P (1975) Cognitive development in adulthood: a fifth stage?, *Developmental Psychology*, 11, pp 602–06

Atchley, R (1993) Critical perspectives on retirement, in *Voices and Visions of Aging: Toward a critical gerontology*, eds T Cole, W Achembaum, P Jakobi and R Kastenbaum, Springer, New York

Bass, S and Caro, F (1995) Older people as researchers: benefits of research to the community, *Educational Gerontology*, 21 (5), pp 467–78

Bauman, Z (1992) *Intimations of Postmodernity*, Routledge, London

Bauman, Z (1993) *Postmodern Ethics*, Blackwell, Oxford

Beck, U (1992) *Risk Society*, tr M Ritter, Sage, London

Beinhart, S and Smith, P (1997) *National Adult Learning Survey 1997*, Department for Education and Employment, London

Belenky, M, Clincy, B, Goldberger, N, Tarule, J (1986) *Women's Ways of Knowing*, Basic Books, New York

Bell, D (1980) *Sociological Journeys: Essays 1960–1980*, London

Benner, P (1984) *From Novice to Expert*, Addison Wesley, California

Berger, P (1969) *The Social Reality of Religion*, Faber and Faber, London

Berger, P and Luckmann, T (1966) *The Social Construction of Reality*, Allen Lane, Penguin Press, London

Bernstein, B (1971) *Class, Codes and Control*, Paladin, London

Birren, J (1963) Psychophysiological relations, in *Human Aging: A biological and behavioral study*, eds J Birren, R Butler, S Greenhouse, L Sokoloff, and M Yarrow, US Government Printing Office, Washington DC

Bohm, D (1985) *Unfolding Meaning*, ARK Paperbacks, London

Boshier, R (1980) Towards a Learning Society, Learning Press, Vancouver

Botwinick, J and Thompson, L (1971) Cardiac functioning and reaction time in relation to age, in *Journal of Geriatric Psychology*, (119), pp 127–32

Bowles, S and Gintis, H (1976) *Schooling in Capitalist America*, Routledge and Kegan Paul, London

Brookfield, S (1990) *The Skillful Teacher*, Jossey Bass, San Francisco

Brookfield, S (1995) *Becoming a Critically Reflective Teacher*, Jossey Bass, San Francisco

Brookfield, S and Preskill, S (1999) *Discussion as a Way of Teaching*, Society for Research into Higher Education and Open University Press, Buckingham

Bryne, E (1995) *Confused States in Older People*, Edward Arnold, London

Buber, M (1959) *I and Thou*, 2nd edn, Clarke, Edinburgh

Buber, M (1961) *Between Man and Man*, Fontana Library, Glasgow

Caldwell, B and Carter, M (1993) *The Return of the Mentor*, Falmer Press, London

Cameron, P (1972) The generation gap: time orientation, *The Gerontologist*, **12** (1), pp 117–19

Campbell, C (1987) *The Romantic Ethic and the Spirit of Modern Consumerism*, Blackwell, Oxford

Campbell, D (1984) *The New Majority: Adult learners in the university*, University of Alberta Press, Edmonton

Carlton, S and Soulsby, J (1999) *Learning to Grow Older and Bolder*, NIACE, Leicester

Carmin, C (1988) Issues on research on mentoring: definitional and methodological, *International Journal of Mentoring*, **2** (2), pp 9–13

Carnegie Inquiry into the Third Age (1993) *Life, Work and Livelihood in the Third Age*, Carnegie United Kingdom Trust, Dunfermline

Caro, F (1999) *Training for Older People in Applied Social Research*, unpublished paper presented to the 1st International Conference on Elder University Programmes, University of Granada, Spain, December

Carruthers, J (1993) The Principles and Practice of Mentoring in The Return of the Mentor, eds B Caldwell and M Carter, Falmer Press, London

Carter, J (1998) *The Virtues of Aging*, Ballentine, New York

Carver, V and Lilliard, P (eds) *An Ageing Population*, Hodder and Stoughton in association with the Open University, Sevenoaks

Cattell, R B (1963) Theory of fluid and crystallized intelligence, *Journal of Educational Psychology*, **54**, pp 1–23

Chène, A (1994) Community-based older learners: being with others, *Educational Gerontology*, 20 (8), pp 65–781

Clark, P (1999) Service-learning education in community-academic partnerships: implications for interdisciplinary geriatric training in the health professions, *Educational Gerontology*, **27** (7), pp 641–60

Clennell, S (ed) (1995) *Training Opportunities for Older Adults*, Open University, Milton Keynes

Clutterbuck, D (1995) *Consenting Adults: Making the most of mentoring*, Channel 4 TV, London

Cochrane, D (1995) *Wisdom*, University of Saskatchewan, Saskatchewan (unpublished essay)

Collins English Dictionary (1979) Collins, Glasgow

Conference Report (1999) *Carry on Learning*, NIACE, Leicester

Coombs, P and Ahmed, M (1974) *Attacking Rural Poverty*, John Hopkins University Press, Baltimore

Cooper, D (1983) *Authenticity and Learning: Nietzsche's educational philosophy*, Routledge, London

Corby, N (1975) Assertiveness training with aged populations, *Counselling Psychologist*, **6** (4), pp 69–74

Cusack, S (1996) Developing a lifelong learning program: empowering seniors in lifelong learning, *Educational Gerontology*, **21** (4), pp 305–20

Cusack, S (1999) Critical educational gerontology and the imperative to empower, *Education and Ageing*, **14** (1), pp 21–37

Cusack, S and Thompson, W (1998) Mental fitness: developing a vital aging society in *International Journal of Lifelong Education*, **17** (5), pp 307–17

Dahlgren, L-O (1984) Outcomes of learning, in *The Experience of Learning*, eds F Marton, D Hounsell and N Entwistle, Scottish University Press, Edinburgh

Daloz, L (1986) *Effective Teaching and Mentoring*, Jossey Bass, San Francisco

Davies, M (1993) Theories of ageing and their implications for pre-retirement education, *Journal of Educational Gerontology*, **8** (2), pp 67–74

Davies, M and James, D (1995) *Seniors as Researchers*, Presentation made to the European Conference on Competence and Productivity in the Third Age, University of Ulm

Davis, R (ed) *My Journey into Dementia*, Scripture Press, Amersham

Dawson, A and Baller, W (1972) Relationships between creative activity and the health of elderly persons, *Journal of Psychology*, **82**, pp 49–58

de Certeau, M (1984) *The Practice of Everyday Life*, University of California Press, Berkeley

Delors, J (1996) *Learning: The treasure within*, UNESCO, Paris

Department for Education and Employment (1998) *The Learning Age*, DfEE, London

Department for Education and Employment (1999) *Learning to Succeed*, DfEE, London

Dewey, J (1938) *Experience and Education*, Collier MacMillan, New York

Dreyfus, S and Dreyfus, H (1980) *A Five Stage Model of the Mental Activities Involved in Directed Skill Acquisition*, unpublished, cited in Benner, P (1984) From Novice to Expert, Addison Wesley, California

Durkheim, E (1956) *Education and Sociology*, The Free Press, New York

Elmore, R (1999) Education for older people: the moral dimension, *Education and Ageing*, **14** (1) pp 9–20

Erikson, E (1950) *Childhood and Society*, Penguin, Harmondsworth

Erikson, E (1965) *Childhood and Society*, rev edn, Penguin, Harmondsworth

European Union (1995) *Teaching and Learning: Towards the learning society*, European Union, Brussels

Featherstone, M and Wernick, A (eds) (1995) *Images of Ageing, Routledge*, London

Fieldhouse, R and Associates (1996) *A History of Modern British Adult Education*, NIACE, Leicester

Foos, P (1997) Effects of memory training on anxiety and performance in older adults, *Educational Gerontology*, **23** (3), pp 243–52

Fowler, J (1981) *Stages of Faith*, Harper and Row, San Francisco

Freire, P (1972) *Pedagogy of the Oppressed*, Penguin, Harmondsworth

Fromm, E (1942) *The Fear of Freedom*, 1984 edn, ARK Paperbacks, London

Fromm, E (1949) *Man for Himself*, Routledge, London

Gardner, H (1983) *Frames of Mind*, Basic Books, New York

Gaskin, K and Smith, J (1995) *A New Civic Europe*, Volunteer Centre, London

Gee, S and Baillie, J (1999) Happily ever after? An exploration of retirement expectations, in *Educational Gerontology*, **25** (2), pp 109–28

Gehlen, A (1988) *Man: His nature and place in the world*, New York, Columbia University Press

Gibson, F (1995) Reaching people with dementia through reminiscence work, in *Reminiscence*, **11**, pp 3–6 (published by Age Exchange, London SE3 9LA)

Giddens, A (1990) *Consequences of Modernity*, Polity Press, Cambridge

Giddens, A (1991) *Modernity and Self-Identity*, Polity Press, Cambridge

Glanz, D and Neikrug, S (unpublished paper) *Seniors and Researchers in the Study of Aging: Learning and doing*

Glover, D and Mardle, G (1995) *The Management of Mentoring*, Kogan Page, London

Goleman, D (1996) *Emotional Intelligence*, Bloomsbury, London

Goleman, D (1998) *Working with Emotional Intelligence*, Bantam Books, New York

Goodman, J (1999) Harvesting a lifetime, in *Spirituality and Ageing*, ed A Jewel, Jessica Kingsley, London

Hanfling, O (1987a) *The Quest for Meaning*, Blackwell in association with the Open University, Oxford

Hanfling, O (1987b) *Life and Meaning*, Blackwell in association with the Open University, Oxford

Hareven, T (1995) Changing images of aging and the social construction of the life course, in *Images of Aging*, eds M Featherstone and A Wernick, pp 119–34, Routledge, London

Harrison, J F C (1961) *Learning and Living 1790–1960*, Routledge and Kegan Paul, London

Hart, M and Horton, D (1993) Beyond God the Father and God the Mother: adult education and spirituality, in *Adult Education and Theological Interpretations*, eds P Jarvis and N Walters, Krieger, Malebar Florida

Harvey, D (1990) The Condition of Postmodernity, Blackwell, Oxford

Havighurst, R (1970) Changing Status and Roles During the Adult Life Cycle, in *Sociological Background to Adult Education*, ed H Burns, Syracuse University, Syracuse

Hawkett, S (1988) *The Philosophy of Terminal Care: Towards a common philosophy and curriculum*, unpublished MSc dissertation, University of Surrey, Guildford

Hearn, J (1995) Imaging the Aging of Men, in *Images of Aging*, eds M Featherstone and A Wernick, pp 97–115, Routledge, London

Heller, A (1984) *Everyday Life*, Routledge and Kegan Paul, London

Hepworth, M (1993) Ageing and the emotions, *Journal of Educational Gerontology*, 8 (2), pp 75–85

Hickson, J and Housley, W (1997) Creativity in later life, *Educational Gerontology*, 26 (3), pp 539–47

Hillman, J et al (1999) Assessing the validity of a social history: intervention to individuate nursing home residents, *Educational Gerontology*, **29** (1), pp 37–50

Horn, J and Cattell, R (1967) Age differences in fluid and crystallized intelligence, *Acta Psychologica*, 26, pp 107–29

Hornstein, G and Wapner, S (1985) Modes of experiencing and adapting to retirement, *International Journal of Aging and Human Development*, **21**, pp 281–315

Houle, C (1984) *Patterns of Learning*, Jossey Bass, San Francisco

Howse, K (1999) *Religion, Spirituality and Older People*, Centre for Policy on Ageing, London

Hudson, F (1999) *The Adult Years*, rev edn, Jossey Bass, San Francisco

Husen, T (1974) *The Learning Society*, Methuen, London

Hutchins, R (1968) *The Learning Society*, Penguin, Harmondsworth

Illich, I (1973) *Deschooling Society*, Penguin, Harmondsworth

Illich, I and Verne, E (1976) *Imprisoned in a Global Classroom*, Writers and Readers Publishing Cooperative, London

Ivy, G, MacLead, C, Petit, T and Markus, J (1992) A physiological framework for perceptual and cognitive changes in aging, in eds F Craik and T Salthouse, *The Handbook of Aging and Cognition*, Lawrence Erlbaum, Hillsdale

James, D and Coyle, C (1998) Physical exercise, IQ scores and working memory in older adult men, *Education and Ageing*, **13** (1), pp 37–48

Jarvis, P (1972) *Religious Socialisation in the Junior School*, University of Birmingham, unpublished MSocSc thesis

Jarvis, P (1980) Pre-retirement education: design and analysis, *Adult Education*, **53** (1), pp 14–19

Jarvis, P (1987) *Adult Learning in the Social Context*, Croom Helm, London

Jarvis, P (1992) *Paradoxes of Learning*, Jossey Bass, San Francisco

Jarvis, P (1995) *Adult and Continuing Education: Theory and practice*, 2nd edn, Routledge, London

Jarvis, P (1996) The public recognition of lifetime learning, *European Journal of Lifelong Learning*, **1**, pp 10–17

Jarvis, P (1997) *Ethics and Education for Adults in Late Modern Society*, NIACE, Leicester

Jarvis, P (1999a) *The Practitioner Researcher*, Jossey Bass, San Francisco

Jarvis, P (1999b) The educational mission of the church to adults: a quest for truth, *Epworth Review*, **26** (1), pp 88–94

Jarvis, P, Dubelaar, J and Joyce, C (1999) *Older People at Work: The elder mentor*, University of Surrey, Guildford

Jewel, A (ed) (1999) *Spirituality and Ageing*, Jessica Kingsley, London

Johnson, J (1993) Does Group Living Work?, eds J Johnson and R Slater, *Ageing and Later Life*, Sage, London

Kant, I (1933) (ed) *Critique of Pure Reason*, Dent, Vermont

Keddie, N (1980) Adult education: an ideology of individualism, in *Adult Education for a Change*, ed J Thompson, Heinemann, London

Kelly, T (1970) *A History of Adult Education in Great Britain*, 2nd edn, Liverpool University Press, Liverpool

Kennedy, H (Chair) (1997) *Learning Works*, Further Education Funding Council, Coventry

Kett, J (1994) *The Pursuit of Knowledge Under Difficulties*, Stanford

Kidd, R (1973) *How Adults Learn*, 2nd edn, Association Press, Chicago

Kirkwood, H (1987) Training for reminiscence work: an example from Scotland, *Journal of Educational Gerontology*, **2** (2), pp 35–45

Kitwood, T (1997) *Dementia Reconsidered*, Open University Press, Buckingham

Knowles, M (1970) *The Modern Practice of Adult Education: Andragogy versus pedagogy*, Association Press, Chicago

Knowles, M (1977) *The Educational Movement in the US*, rev edn, Robert Krieger, New York

Knowles, M (1980) *The Modern Practice of Adult Education: From pedagogy to andragogy*, rev edn, Association Press, Chicago

Knox, A (1977) *Adult Development and Learning*, Jossey Bass, San Francisco

Knudson, R (1979) Andragogy revisited: humanagogy anyone?, *Adult Education*, **29**, pp 261–64

Koestler, A (1964) *The Act of Creation*, Dell, New York

Kohlberg, L (1986) *The Philosophy of Moral Development*, Harper and Row, San Francisco

Kolb, D (1984) *Experiential Learning*, Prentice Hall, Englewood Cliffs, NJ

Label, J (1978) Beyond andragogy to gerogogy, *Lifelong Learning: The adult years*, 1

Labouvie-Vief, G (1985) Models of cognitive functioning in the old adult: research needs in educational gerontology, in *Introduction to Educational Gerontology*, 2nd edn, eds R Sherron and D B Lumsdon, Hemisphere Publishing, Washington

Lengrand, P (1975) *An Introduction to Lifelong Education*, Croom Helm, London

Levinas, E (1991) *Totality and Infinity*, Kluwer, Dordrecht

Levinson, D with Darrow, C, Klien, E, Levinson, M and McKee, B (1978) *The Seasons of a Man's Life*, Knorf, New York

Levinson, D with Levinson, J (1996) *The Season's of a Woman's Life*, Ballentine, New York

Loevinger, J (1976) *Ego Development*, Jossey Bass, San Francisco

Long, H and Associates (1998) *Developing Paradigms for Self-Directed Learning*, College of Education, University of Oklahoma

Luce, G (1979) *Your Second Life: Vitality and growth in middle and later years*, Delacorte, New York

Luckmann, T (1967) *Invisible Religion*, MacMillan, London

Lyotard, J-F (1984) *The Postmodern Condition: A report on knowledge*, Manchester University Press, Manchester

Lyotard, J-F (1992) *The Postmodern Explained to Children*, Turnaround, London

McIntyre, D, Hagger, H and Wilkin, M (1993) *Mentoring*, Kogan Page, London

McIsaac, S (1996) Communicating with the 'confused': educational implications of the interactivist perspective, *Education and Ageing*, 11 (1), pp 44–58

MacMurray, J (1961) *Persons in Relation*, Humanities Press, New Jersey

Macquarrie, J (1973) *Existentialism*, Pelican, Harmondsworth

Mangrum, F and Mangrum, C (1995) An ethnomethodological study of concerted and biographical work performed by elderly persons during game playing, *Educational Gerontology*, 21 (3), pp 231–46

Marcel, G (1976) *Being and Having*, Peter Smith, Gloucester, Mass

Marcus, G (1992) Past, present and emergent identities: requirements for ethnographies of late twentieth-century modernity worldwide, in *Modernity and Identity*, eds S Lash and J Friedman, Blackwell, Oxford

Marsick, V and Watkins, K (1990) *Informal and Incidental Learning in the Workplace*, Routledge, London

Maslow, A (1964) *Towards a Psychology of Being*, 2nd edn, Van Nostrand Reinhold, New York

Megginson, D and Clutterbuck, D (1995) *Mentoring in Action*, Kogan Page, London

Merriam, S (1985) Reminiscence and life review: the potential for educational intervention, in *Introduction to Educational Gerontology*, 2nd edn, eds R Sherron and B Lumsden, Hemisphere, Washington

Merriam, S and Caffarella, R (1991) *Learning in Adulthood*, Jossey Bass, San Francisco

Merriam, S and Cross, L (1981) Aging, reminiscence and life satisfaction, *Activities, Adaptation and Aging*, **2**, pp 39–50

Mezirow, J (1988) Transformation theory, *Proceedings of the 29th Annual Adult Education Research Conference*, Faculty of Continuing Education, University of Calgary, Calgary

Mezirow, J (1991) *Transformative Dimensions of Adult Learning*, Jossey Bass, San Francisco

Moody, H (1986) Education and the Life Cycle, in *Education and Aging*, eds D Peterson, J Thornton and J Birren, Prentice Hall, Englewood Cliffs, NJ

Moody, H (1998) *Aging: Concepts and controversies*, 2nd edn, Pine Forge, Thousand Oaks, CA

Moore, P (1999) The Lifespan Challenge, *RSA Journal*, (3/4), pp 58–61

Morton-Cooper, A and Palmer, A (1993) *Mentoring and Preceptorship*, Blackwell, Oxford

Moshman, D (1979) To really get ahead, get a metatheory, in *Intellectual Development beyond Childhood*, ed D Kuhn, Jossey Bass, San Francisco

Murphy, E (1993) Depression in later life, in *Ageing and Later Life*, eds J Johnson and R Slater, Sage, London

Murray, M with Owen, M (1991) *Beyond the Myths and Magic of Mentoring*, Jossey Bass, San Francisco

Neugarten, B (1977) Adult personality: towards a psychology of the life cycle, in *Readings in Adult Psychology: Contemporary Perspectives*, eds T Allman and D Jaffe, Harper, New York

Niebuhr Jr, H (1984) *Revitalizing American Learning*, Wadsworth, Belmont

Nielsen, E and Thyssen, S (1993) *Existence and Care*, Danish National Institute for Educational Research for the Mind in Later Life, Copenhagen

Nyiri, J (1988) Tradition and practical knowledge, in *Practical Knowledge*, eds J Nyiri and P Smith, Croom Helm, London

Oakeshott, M (1933) *Modes of Experience*, Cambridge University Press, Cambridge

Organisation for Economic Cooperation and Development (1996) *Lifelong Learning for All*, OECD, Paris

Osmond, N (1995) Life after stroke: special interest book writing groups, in *Engaging with Difference*, eds M Stewart and A Thomson, pp 173–86, NIACE, Leicester

Paggi, K and Hayslip, B (1999) Mental aerobics: exercises for the mind in later life, in *Educational Gerontology*, 25 (1)

Panayotoff, K (1993) Impact of continuing education on the health of older adults, *Educational Gerontology*, **19** (1), pp 9–20

Peters, R (1966) *Ethics and Education*, Allen and Unwin, London

Phillipson, C (1998) *Reconstructing Old Age*, Sage, London

Phillipson, C and Strang, P (1983) *The Impact of Pre-Retirement Education*, Dept of Adult Education, University of Keele

Piaget, J (1929) *The Child's Conception of the World*, Routledge and Kegan Paul, London

Pineau, G (1995) Life histories considered as an art of existence, in *The Biographical Approach in European Adult Education*, eds Alheit P et al, pp 44–56, Verband Wiener Volksbilgung, Vienna

Polanyi, M (1962) *Personal Knowledge*, Routledge and Kegan Paul, London

Prager, E (1995) The older volunteer as research colleague: toward 'generative participation' for older adults, in *Educational Gerontology*, **21** (3), pp 209–18

Ranson, S (1994) *Towards the Learning Society*, Cassell, London

Reason, P and Rowan, J (1981) *Human Inquiry*, John Wiley and Sons, Chichester

Reich, R (1991) *The Work of Nations*, Simon and Schuster, London

Riegel, K (1979) *Foundations of Dialectic Psychology*, Academic Press, London

Rodin, J and Langer, E (1977) Long-term effects of a control-relevant intervention with the institutionalized aged, *Journal of Personality and Social Psychology*, 35, pp 897–902

Rogers, C (1961) *On Becoming a Person*, Constable, London

Rogers, C (1969) *Freedom to Learn*, Columbus, Merrill, Ohio

Rosow, I (1967) *Social Integration of the Aged*, Free Press, New York

Saunders, C (1978) Care of the dying, in *An Ageing Population*, eds V Carver and P Lilliard, Hodder and Stoughton in association with Open University Press, Sevenoaks

Scheler, M (1980) *Problems of a Sociology of Knowledge*, tr M Frings, ed K Stikkers, Routledge and Kegan Paul, London

Schon, D (1983) *The Reflective Practitioner*, Basic Books, New York

Schutz, A (1932/1967) *The Phenomenology of the Social World*, Heinemann, London

Schutz, A and Luckmann, T (1974) *The Structures of the Lifeworld*, Heinemann, London

Sheehy, G (1995) *New Life Passages*, Random House of Canada, Canada

Stehr, N (1994) *Knowledge Societies*, Sage, London

Stone, N (1992) Consumers and an evaluation of day care provision: an occupational therapist's perspective, *Journal of Educational Gerontology*, **7** (2), pp 92–105

Strauss, A (ed) (1964) *George Herbert Mead on Social Psychology*, University of Chicago Press, Chicago

Strom, R and Strom, S (1995) Intergenerational learning: grandparents in schools, *Educational Gerontology*, 21 (4), pp 321–36

Strom, R *et al* (1997) Cooperative learning in old age: instruction and assessment, *Educational Gerontology*, **23** (6), pp 581–99

Sutton, L (1995) *Whose Memory is it Anyway?*, University of Southampton, unpublished PhD thesis

Thompson, J (1983) *Learning Liberation*, Croom Helm, London

Thornton, J (1986) Lifespan learning and education, in Education and Aging, eds D Peterson, J Thornton and J Birren, Prentice Hall, Englewood Cliffs, NJ

Tough, A (1972) *The Adult's Learning Projects*, 2nd edn, Ontario Institute for Studies in Education, Toronto

Truluck, J and Courtenay, B (1999) Learning style preferences among older adults, *Educational Gerontology*, **25** (3), pp 221–36

Turner, B (1991) *Religion and Social Theory*, 2nd edn, Sage, London

Turner, V (1974) *The Ritual Process*, Penguin, Harmondsworth

Usher, R and Edwards, R (1994) *Education and Postmodernism*, Routledge, London

Vaillant, G (1993) *The Wisdom of the Ego*, Harvard University Press, Cambridge Mass

van Gennep, A (1908) *The Rites of Passage*, Routledge and Kegan Paul, London

Waters, E and Goodman, J (1990) *Empowering Older Adults*, Jossey Bass, San Francisco

Wilcock, P (1999) Death and the spirituality of ageing, in *Spirituality and Ageing*, ed A Jewell, Jessica Kingsley, London

Wildemeersch, D and Jansen, T (1992) *Adult Education, Experiential Learning and Social Change*, VTA Groep, Driebergen

Wilson, P (1999) Memory, personhood and faith, in *Spirituality and Ageing*, ed A Jewell, Jessica Kingsley, London

Worrall, L *et al* (1998) An evaluation of the '*Keep on Talking*' programme for maintaining communication skills into old age, *Educational Gerontology*, **24** (2), pp 129–40

Worsley, R (1996) *Age and Employment*, Age Concern England, London

Yeaxlee, B (1925) *Spiritual Values in Adult Education*, Oxford University Press, London (2 vols)

Yeaxlee, B (1929) *Lifelong Education*, Cassell, London

Ylanne-McEwen, V (1999) Discourses of Age Identity in Travel Agency Interaction, *Ageing and Society*, **19**, part 4, pp 417–40

Young, F (1999) *Recovering the Wisdom of the Past for the 21st Century*, Hugh Price Hughes lecture delivered at Hinde Street Methodist Church, Hugh Price, London

Zohar, D and Marshall, I (2000) *Spiritual Intelligence: The ultimate intelligence*, Bloomsbury, London

Index